ECONOMIC ISSUES, PROBLEMS AND PERSPECTIVES

CHARITABLE ORGANIZATIONS

IRS OVERSIGHT AND TAX ISSUES FOR CONGRESS

ECONOMIC ISSUES, PROBLEMS AND PERSPECTIVES

Additional books in this series can be found on Nova's website under the Series tab.

Additional e-books in this series can be found on Nova's website under the e-book tab.

ECONOMIC ISSUES, PROBLEMS AND PERSPECTIVES

CHARITABLE ORGANIZATIONS

IRS OVERSIGHT AND TAX ISSUES FOR CONGRESS

LYNDA MEYERS
EDITOR

New York

Library of Congress Cataloging-in-Publication Data

ISBN: 978-1-63482-600-6

Published by Nova Science Publishers, Inc. † New York

CONTENTS

PREFACE

This book describes the charitable organization sector; describes IRS oversight activities; determines how IRS assesses its oversight efforts; and determines how IRS collaborates with state charity regulators and U.S. Attorneys to identify and prosecute organizations suspected of engaging in fraudulent (or other criminal) activity. This book also provides an overview of recent changes affecting tax-exempt and charitable organizations, while also discussing issues that may be of legislative interest in the future.

Chapter 1 – IRS oversight of charitable organizations helps to ensure they abide by the purposes that justify their tax exemption and protects the sector from potential abuses and loss of confidence by the donor community. In recent years, reductions in IRS's budget have raised concerns about the adequacy of IRS oversight.

GAO was asked to review IRS oversight of charitable organizations. In this report, GAO (1) describes the charitable organization sector, (2) describes IRS oversight activities, (3) determines how IRS assesses its oversight efforts, and (4) determines how IRS collaborates with state charity regulators and U.S. Attorneys to identify and prosecute organizations suspected of engaging in fraudulent (or other criminal) activity.

GAO reviewed and analyzed IRS data, strategic planning and performance documents, and documented improvement efforts. We also interviewed IRS and Department of Justice officials, state charity regulators, and subject matter specialists. GAO compared IRS's practices to federal guidance on performance management.

Chapter 2 – Prior to the financial crises and subsequent recession, the value of tax benefits for charitable contributions and organizations was estimated to be around $100 billion per year. About half of this cost arose from the deductions for charitable contributions with the other half from exemptions of earnings of nonprofits. In 2010, the deduction for charitable contributions resulted in an estimated $40 billion in federal revenue losses. On average, endowment investments in 2009 experienced losses, meaning that the federal government did not lose revenues from exempting asset returns from taxation. By 2011, these returns on endowments almost recovered to their prior levels, although they fell to approximately zero for 2012. Over the longer run, however, they are likely to earn a substantial return.

This report provides an overview of recent changes affecting tax-exempt and charitable organizations, while also discussing issues that may be of legislative interest in the future. The Pension Protection Act (P.L. 109-280) included a number of restrictions related to charitable contributions as well as restrictions on tax-exempt organizations. These changes are briefly surveyed.

In addition to changes regarding the treatment of charitable contributions and tax-exempt organizations that have been made in recent years, several issues may be considered in future legislation. A number of provisions related to charitable contributions were extended temporarily as part of the tax extenders in the American Taxpayer Relief Act of 2012 (P.L. 112-240). Most of the charitable extenders were contained in legislation first introduced in 2001. Some provisions were enacted temporarily in 2005; further provisions and extensions occurred in 2006, in the Pension Protection Act. These extenders include an individual retirement account (IRA) rollover, liberalized treatment of gifts of food inventory and conservation property, and two more technical provisions. Limitations on itemized deductions have been proposed as part of the Fiscal Commission's recommendation. President Obama's budgets have proposed limiting itemized deductions' value, including charitable contributions, to 28%. Other types of limits may be considered as part of tax reform. The Patient Protection and Affordable Care Act (PPACA; P.L. 111-148), in response to concerns regarding charity care and community benefits provided by tax-exempt hospitals, imposed new regulations.

Other issues that may arise reflect concerns about donor-advised funds and supporting organizations and educational institutions' endowments. For donor-advised funds and supporting organizations, the main issue is whether and how minimum distribution requirements should be imposed, alongside other new regulations. The decline in educational institutions' endowments had raised concerns that such declines may lead to tuition increases, although these assets have largely recovered. New reporting requirements for small tax-exempt organizations, enacted under the Pension Protection Act (P.L. 109-280) may cause a number of noncompliant tax-exempt entities to lose their tax-exempt status.

In: Charitable Organizations
Editor: Lynda Meyers
ISBN: 978-1-63482-600-6

Chapter 1

Tax-Exempt Organizations: Better Compliance Indicators and Data, and More Collaboration with State Regulators Would Strengthen Oversight of Charitable Organizations*

United States Government Accountability Office

Why GAO Did This Study

IRS oversight of charitable organizations helps to ensure they abide by the purposes that justify their tax exemption and protects the sector from potential abuses and loss of confidence by the donor community. In recent years, reductions in IRS's budget have raised concerns about the adequacy of IRS oversight.

GAO was asked to review IRS oversight of charitable organizations. In this report, GAO (1) describes the charitable organization sector, (2) describes IRS oversight activities, (3) determines how IRS assesses its oversight efforts, and (4) determines how IRS collaborates with state charity regulators and U.S.

* This is an edited, reformatted and augmented version of a United States Government Accountability Office publication, No. GAO-15-164, dated December 2014.

Attorneys to identify and prosecute organizations suspected of engaging in fraudulent (or other criminal) activity.

GAO reviewed and analyzed IRS data, strategic planning and performance documents, and documented improvement efforts. We also interviewed IRS and Department of Justice officials, state charity regulators, and subject matter specialists. GAO compared IRS's practices to federal guidance on performance management.

WHAT GAO RECOMMENDS

GAO recommends IRS 1) develop compliance goals and additional performance measures that can be used to assess the impact of enforcement activities on compliance and 2) clearly communicate with state charity regulators how they are allowed to use IRS information related to examinations of charitable organizations. GAO also recommends that Congress consider expanding the mandate for 501(c)(3) organizations to electronically file their tax returns to cover a greater share of filed returns. In written comments, IRS agreed with GAO's recommendations.

WHAT GAO FOUND

Charitable organizations play a major role in our economy and provide critical services and resources to families and individuals in need. Although charitable organizations vary considerably in size and purpose, in 2011 the largest number of organizations was in the human services sector, providing services such as employment and housing assistance. The highest concentration of assets was in the health and education sectors, which include hospitals and universities. In addition to being concentrated in a few sectors, a large proportion of all assets were controlled by a relatively small number of charitable organizations—less than 3 percent hold more than 80 percent of the assets.

Over the past several years, as the Internal Revenue Service (IRS) budget has declined, the number of full-time equivalents (FTEs) within its Exempt Organizations (EO) division has fallen, leading to a steady decrease in the number of charitable organizations examined. In 2011, the examination rate was 0.81 percent; in 2013, it fell to 0.71 percent. This rate is lower than the exam rate for other types of taxpayers, such as individuals (1.0 percent) and corporations (1.4 percent).

EO is grappling with several challenges that complicate oversight efforts. While EO has some compliance information, such as how often exams result in change of tax exempt status, it does not have quantitative measures of compliance for the charitable sector as a whole, for specific segments of the sector (such as universities and hospitals) or for particular aspects of noncompliance (such as personal inurement or political activity). Because EO does not have these measures and does not know the current level of compliance, it cannot set quantitative, results-oriented goals for increasing compliance or assess to what extent its actions are affecting compliance.

Statutory requirements for safeguarding taxpayer data limit both IRS's ability to share data and state regulators' ability to use it. A lack of clarity about how state regulators are allowed to use IRS data to build cases against suspect charitable organizations further impedes regulators' ability to leverage IRS's examination work.

The e-filing rate for tax-exempt organizations is significantly lower than for other taxpayers. This lower rate means there is less digitized data available for data analytics and higher labor costs for IRS. Expanded e-filing may result in more accurate and complete data becoming available in a timelier manner, which in turn, would allow IRS to more easily identify areas of noncompliance.

ABBREVIATIONS

ACT	Advisory Committee on Tax Exempt and Government Entities
DOJ	Department of Justice
EO	Exempt Organizations
FTE	full-time equivalent
GDP	gross domestic product
GPRA	Government Performance and Results Act of 1993
IRC	Internal Revenue Code
IRS	Internal Revenue Service
MOU	memorandum of understanding
NAAG	National Association of Attorneys General
NASCO	National Association of State Charity Officials
NRP	National Research Program

PPA	Pension Protection Act of 2006
RICS	Return Inventory Classification System
SOI	Statistics of Income
TIGTA	Treasury Inspector General for Tax Administration
Treasury	Department of the Treasury

* * *

December 17, 2014

The Honorable Tom Coburn, M.D.
Ranking Member
Committee on Homeland Security and Governmental Affairs
United States Senate

Dear Dr. Coburn:

The breadth and diversity of the tax-exempt sector, which encompasses over 1.6 million entities, including 501(c)(3) charitable organizations, allows it to address a wide range of needs, including comfort to the aging, and food, shelter and other services for families and individuals in need.[1] Moreover, the tax-exempt sector represents an estimated 5 percent of gross domestic product and is concentrated in two key sectors of the economy, with the largest assets in healthcare and education. The Internal Revenue Service (IRS), along with the states, has a vital role in overseeing the tax-exempt sector. IRS oversight can help ensure that exempt entities abide by the purposes that justify their tax exemption. IRS can also help protect the sector from potential abuses and loss of confidence by the donor community that could result from the abusive activities of a small minority of charitable organizations.

IRS—which oversees charitable organizations' compliance with the tax code—has experienced budget cuts over the past several years. As we previously reported, the IRS budget has declined by about $900 million since fiscal year 2010 and funding is below fiscal year 2009 levels.[2] Staffing has also declined by about 10,000 full-time equivalents (FTE) since fiscal year 2010, and performance has been uneven. Questions about the impact of budget cuts on IRS's operations have raised concerns about the adequacy of oversight of charitable organizations.

You asked us to review a number of issues related to the IRS oversight of charitable organizations. This report (1) describes what is known about the number, type, size, and other characteristics of charitable organizations; (2) describes IRS oversight activities for charitable organizations; (3) determines how IRS assesses its oversight efforts of charitable organizations to ensure they are meeting their charitable purposes; and (4) determines how IRS collaborates with state charity regulators and U.S. Attorneys to identify and prosecute organizations suspected of engaging in fraudulent or other criminal activity.

To address the first objective, we reviewed IRS documentation and analyzed data from IRS's Statistics of Income (SOI) samples of tax-exempt organization information returns for tax year 2011, the most recent year available.[3] We used data from the charitable organizations that filed Forms 990 and 990-EZ (which provide information on the filing organization's mission, programs, and finances). We do not report data on private foundations (which are charitable organizations that file Form 990-PF) or report data on Form 990-N filers, because the data for these organizations is less complete and has other limitations. In addition, our data excludes certain religious organizations, which qualify as 501(c)(3) organizations, but are not required to file a return. The SOI samples were based on returns as filed, and did not reflect IRS audit results. The data that we report are estimates based on the SOI sample; statements about sampling errors are reported in appendix III.

For the second objective, we reviewed IRS documentation and obtained IRS data on IRS oversight activities including referrals and examinations performed on charitable organizations, and reviewed data on charitable organizations that had their tax-exempt statuses revoked for fiscal years 2011 through 2013. We also interviewed IRS officials about their oversight activities.

To assess the reliability of the data we analyzed, we reviewed IRS documentation and interviewed agency officials familiar with the data. We determined that these data were sufficiently reliable for the purposes of this report.

For the third objective, we reviewed relevant strategic and performance documents and interviewed IRS planning officials and division managers to determine the extent to which managers overseeing the tax-exempt sector do the following: set performance goals, develop measures to monitor their progress toward meeting goals, and use data both to identify challenges and their causes, and to develop strategies to address those challenges. We reviewed past recommendations made by the Treasury Inspector General for Tax Administration (TIGTA) and the National Taxpayer Advocate related to performance management and interviewed IRS managers about how they addressed the issues discussed in those reports. For criteria, we compared IRS information on performance measures and decision making to *Standards for Internal Control in the Federal Government* and federal guidance on performance management.[4] We also applied the criteria concerning the administration, compliance burden, and transparency that characterize a good tax system, as developed in our guide for evaluating tax reform proposals.[5]

To determine how IRS collaborates with state charity regulators and U.S. Attorneys, we reviewed various IRS documents and interviewed IRS and Department of Justice (DOJ) officials, and representatives from National Association of State Charity Officials (NASCO). For criteria, we identified different approaches for sharing information and collaboration, based on our audit findings, as well as our past recommendations and recommendations made by the Advisory Committee on Tax Exempt and Government Entities (ACT).[6]

To provide additional context for all three objectives, we interviewed IRS officials, DOJ officials, state charity regulators, subject matter specialists, and stakeholder groups representing different types of exempt-organizations and private watchdog organizations that oversee charities about the following: the adequacy of IRS oversight of charitable organizations, the challenges IRS faces providing effective oversight, and strategies to address those challenges.

We conducted this performance audit from June 2014 to December 2014 in accordance with generally accepted government auditing standards. Those standards require that we plan and perform the audit to obtain sufficient, appropriate evidence to provide a reasonable basis for our findings and conclusions based on our audit objectives. We believe that the evidence obtained provides a reasonable basis for our findings and conclusions based on our audit objectives. More detailed information on our scope and methodology appears in appendix I.

BACKGROUND

Section 501 of the Internal Revenue Code (IRC) provides for tax exemption for certain corporations, trusts, and other organizations. Section 501(c) establishes 29 categories of tax-exempt organizations, ranging from cemeteries to professional football leagues—see appendix II for complete list of different types of tax-exempt-organizations, as well as more detailed information on the tax treatment for these organizations. The largest number of such organizations falls under section 501(c)(3), which recognizes charitable organizations. Generally, while charitable organizations pay no income taxes on contributions received, these entities can be taxed on income generated from business activities that are unrelated to their charitable purposes. These charitable organizations and related parties may be subject to several additional IRS penalties and fines for certain actions, such as not filing a required tax return. Generally, taxpayers who itemize their deductions may deduct the amount of any contribution to charitable organizations from their taxable income.

The IRC requires that an organization adhere to certain accepted charitable, religious, educational, scientific, or literary purposes to qualify for 501(c)(3) tax-exempt status.[7] The IRC also prohibits charitable organizations from undertaking certain activities: no earnings of the organization may benefit individual or private shareholders, no substantial attempt may be made to spread propaganda or influence legislation, and no effort may be made to campaign for or against a candidate for public office.[8] In order to receive 501(c)(3) tax-exempt status, an organization must submit a Form 1023 or Form 1023-EZ and organizing documents to IRS to describe its charitable purpose and financial data.[9] The organizing documents can include articles of incorporation or by-laws governing the activities and charitable purpose of the entity. Submitting an application is one of the first interactions a tax-exempt organization will have with IRS.[10] The organization will then receive a determination letter from IRS which informs the organization whether its application for tax-exempt status has been approved or denied. Alternatively, the organization may be told the IRS is in need of additional information in order to make a determination.

If an organization is successful in receiving tax-exempt status, it will continue to interact with IRS on an annual basis by submitting an information return or an electronic notice.[11] The form contains information on the organization's mission, programs, finances and governance structure which helps IRS to determine whether the organization is meeting its charitable purpose and therefore is eligible for tax-exempt status. Certain organizations that have gross receipts of $50,000 per year or less may submit the Form 990-N—an abbreviated electronic version of the Form 990 return, often called the e-Postcard. The Form 990-EZ is less abbreviated, though still more streamlined than the Form 990, and may be used by certain entities with gross receipts under $200,000 and assets under $500,000. Private foundations complete the 990-PF.[12]

Table 1. Information Returns Filed by 501(c)(3) Tax-Exempt Organizations

Form	Description	Threshold
990	The Form 990 is an information return submitted to IRS by organizations exempt from income tax. This form includes information on an entity's mission, programs, finances, and corporate governance structure. Organizations that are required to submit the Form 990 must submit this form annually.	Gross receipts greater than or equal to $200,000 or total assets greater than or equal to $500,000.
990-EZ	A streamlined version of the Form 990, which may be used by entities with gross receipts under $200,000 and assets under $500,000. Organizations eligible to file a Form 990-EZ may choose to file the Form 990.	Gross receipts less than $200,000 and total assets less than $500,000.
990-N	Also called the e-Postcard, this is an abbreviated version of the Form 990 for entities with gross receipts of $50,000 per year or less. This form is submitted electronically. Organizations eligible to file a Form 990-N may choose to file the Forms 990-EZ or 990.	Gross receipts normally less than or equal to $50,000.
990-PF	This Form 990 is used by private foundations regardless of their financial status. Private foundations may not use other versions of the Form 990.	Regardless of financial status.

Source: GAO analysis of IRS forms. | GAO-15-164

IRS oversees charitable organizations through its Exempt Organizations (EO) Business Division (a part of IRS's Tax Exempt and Government Entities Division). EO's oversight relies primarily on two sets of activities: a front-end review of applications and a back-end review of a relatively small number of information and tax returns. At the front end, the EO Rulings and Agreements office reviews all applications for tax-exempt status. At the back end, EO Examinations analyzes the operations and finances of a small percentage of exempt organizations through examinations (audits). Exam agents propose tax assessments or changes to exempt status when necessary, as well as advise organizations about how to comply with the law in the future. Through these activities, IRS tries to ensure that charities merit the recognition of a tax-exempt status as well as the retention of it.[13]

IRS and state charity regulators both play a key role providing oversight of charitable organizations.[14] IRS's oversight interests are in ensuring that tax-exempt organizations comply with federal tax law. State charity regulators have a broader oversight interest which includes the application of state trust, non-profit corporation, consumer protection, and charitable solicitation laws. Although these federal and state regulators have distinct oversight interests, these interests are closely related and at times, overlapping. Both IRS and state charity regulators seek to prevent excess compensation, private inurement, conflicts of interest, and other abusive practices by charitable organizations. IRS also collaborates with U.S. Attorneys at the DOJ to identify and prosecute criminal tax violations. Although EO does not collaborate directly with DOJ, criminal investigations may be initiated within IRS at the recommendation of an IRS revenue agent who has detected potential criminal activity. Investigations may also be initiated at the advice of a U.S. Attorney's office, a law enforcement agency, or the public. IRS criminal investigations are led by an IRS special agent. If substantial evidence is found for a criminal case, then—after multiple rounds of supervisory review—the investigation may be referred to the DOJ Tax Division or the relevant U.S. Attorney's office. If DOJ or the U.S. Attorney accepts the investigation for prosecution, the case is then handled by the prosecutors.[15]

Charitable Organizations Comprise a Major Part of Our Economy and Vary Considerably in Size and Purpose

Charitable organizations comprise a significant part of our economy in terms of their share of the gross domestic product (GDP) and their importance in services vital to the well being of citizens. Available estimates indicate that tax-exempt organizations serving households generate about 5 percent of U.S. GDP.[16] The federal government increasingly relies on these organizations to deliver critical services: in 2012, government agencies paid an estimated $137 billion to nonprofit organizations in grants and contracts for services.[17] Also, for fiscal year 2013, the Department of the Treasury (Treasury) estimated the tax expenditure for deductions for contributions to charitable organizations totaled over $48 billion.[18]

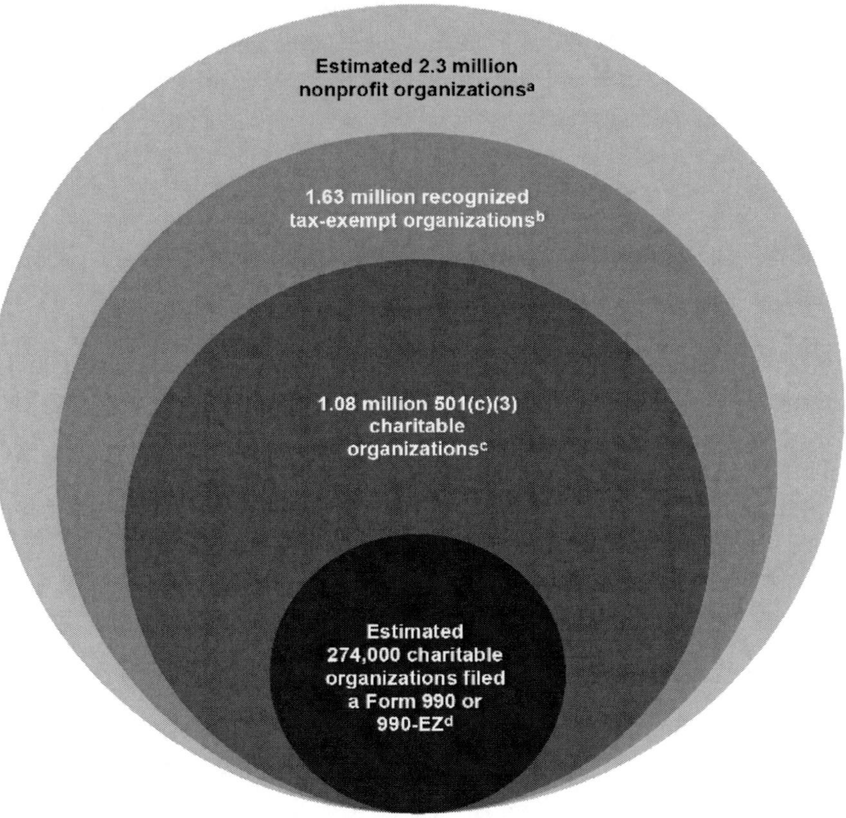

Source: GAO analysis. | GAO-15-164.

[a]This is an estimate of the total number of nonprofit organizations in the United States, including those that have not applied for or received tax-exempt status from IRS. This data is from Urban Institute's *The Nonprofit Almanac 2012*. The almanac did not have 2011 data for the universe of estimated nonprofit organizations, but we would not expect the number to vary greatly between 2011 and 2012.

[b]This includes all organizations that have been recognized as tax-exempt by IRS. The data is from the *IRS Data Book 2011*.[22]

[c]This includes all organizations that are tax-exempt 501(c)(3) charitable organizations. The data is from the *IRS Data Book 2011*.

[d]This is an estimate of all 501(c)(3) charitable organizations that filed Forms 990 or 990-EZ. This figure excludes other types of tax-exempt entities that may have filled these forms. This also excludes 501(c)(3) charitable organizations that filed Forms 990-N or 990-PF, or a different type of return. This is a GAO analysis of SOI data for tax year 2011.

Figure 1. The Universe of Nonprofit Organizations.

As shown in figure 1, the total population of nonprofit organizations can be broken down by tax-exempt status and by the requirement to file returns.[19] In 2012, an estimated 2.3 million nonprofit organizations operated in the United States, including organizations that have not applied for tax-exempt status with IRS.[20] Of nonprofits in 2011, 1.63 million had been recognized as tax-exempt by IRS and 1.08 million of them were 501(c)(3) charitable organizations.[21] An estimated 274,000 of these charitable organizations filed returns—around 189,000 filed Form 990 and 85,000 filed Form 990-EZ.

As shown in figure 2, the number of charitable organizations that were recognized as tax-exempt by IRS increased from more than 960,000 in 2003 to more than 1.28 million in 2010 (a 33 percent increase) but declined to 1.05 million in 2013 (a 18 percent decrease from 2010). After 2010, this decline was primarily due to the Pension Protection Act of 2006 (PPA), which mandated that any organization—large or small—that failed to file a required return or notice for three consecutive years would automatically lose its federal tax exemption.[23] Since PPA's passage, more than 570,000 organizations have lost their tax-exempt status through the automatic revocation process.[24] The net effect on the number of charitable organizations (when new applicants and reinstated revocations are included) is an average decline of about 200,000 from the peak in 2010.

Although Charitable Organizations Vary in Size and Purpose, a Small Number Concentrated in the Health and Education Sectors Control Most Assets

Charitable organizations, excluding private foundations, represent a diverse array of mission areas and range greatly in asset size, the amount of revenue they raise, and their expenses. As shown in figure 3, the largest number of charitable organizations filing Forms 990 and 990- EZ were in the human services sector. However, the health and education sectors had the largest amount of assets.

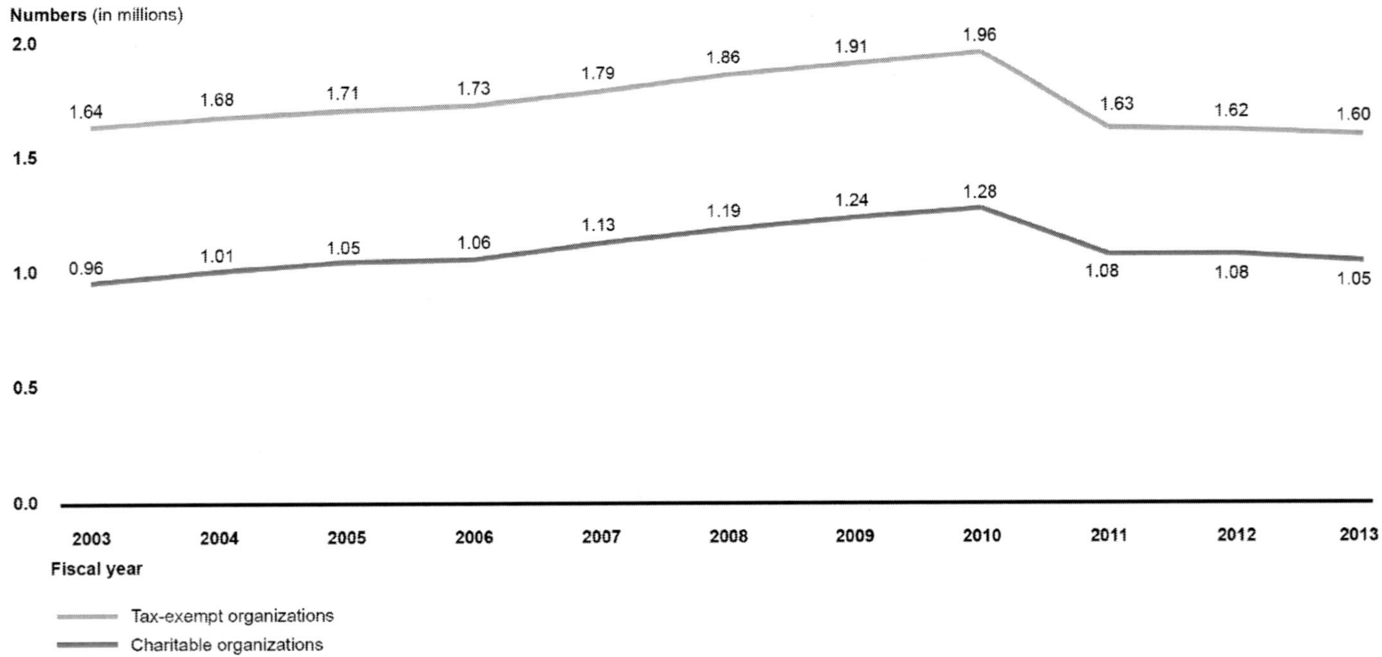

Source: IRS Data Books. | GAO-15-164.

Note: Includes private foundations. For fiscal year 2013, cooperative hospital service organizations, cooperative service organizations of operating educational organizations, child care organizations, and charitable risk pools were reported with section 501(c)(3) charitable organizations.

Figure 2. Number of Tax-Exempt and Charitable Organizations That Were Recognized As Tax-Exempt from IRS, Fiscal Years 2003-2013.

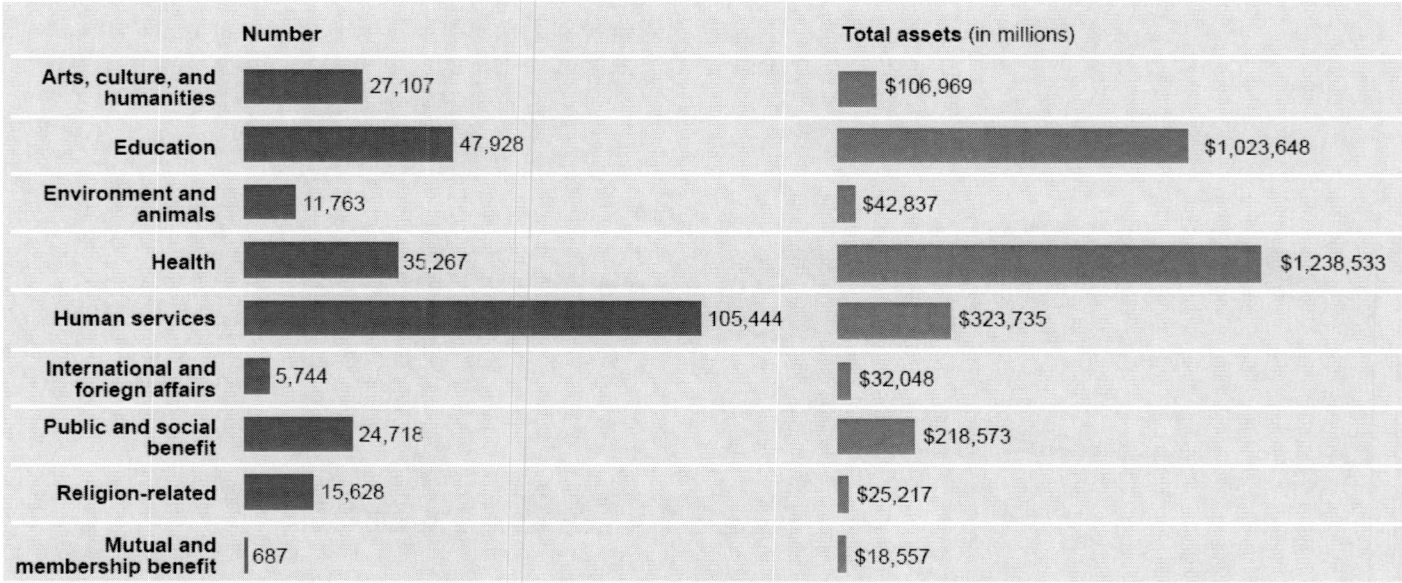

Sources: GAO analysis of SOI data from IRS Form 990 and IRS Form 990-EZ; PhotoDisc (images). | GAO-15-164

Note: Statements about sampling errors are reported in appendix III. See Tables 6 and 7 in Appendix III for further data used in Figure 3.

Figure 3. Number of Charitable Organization Filers by Mission Category, Tax Year 2011.

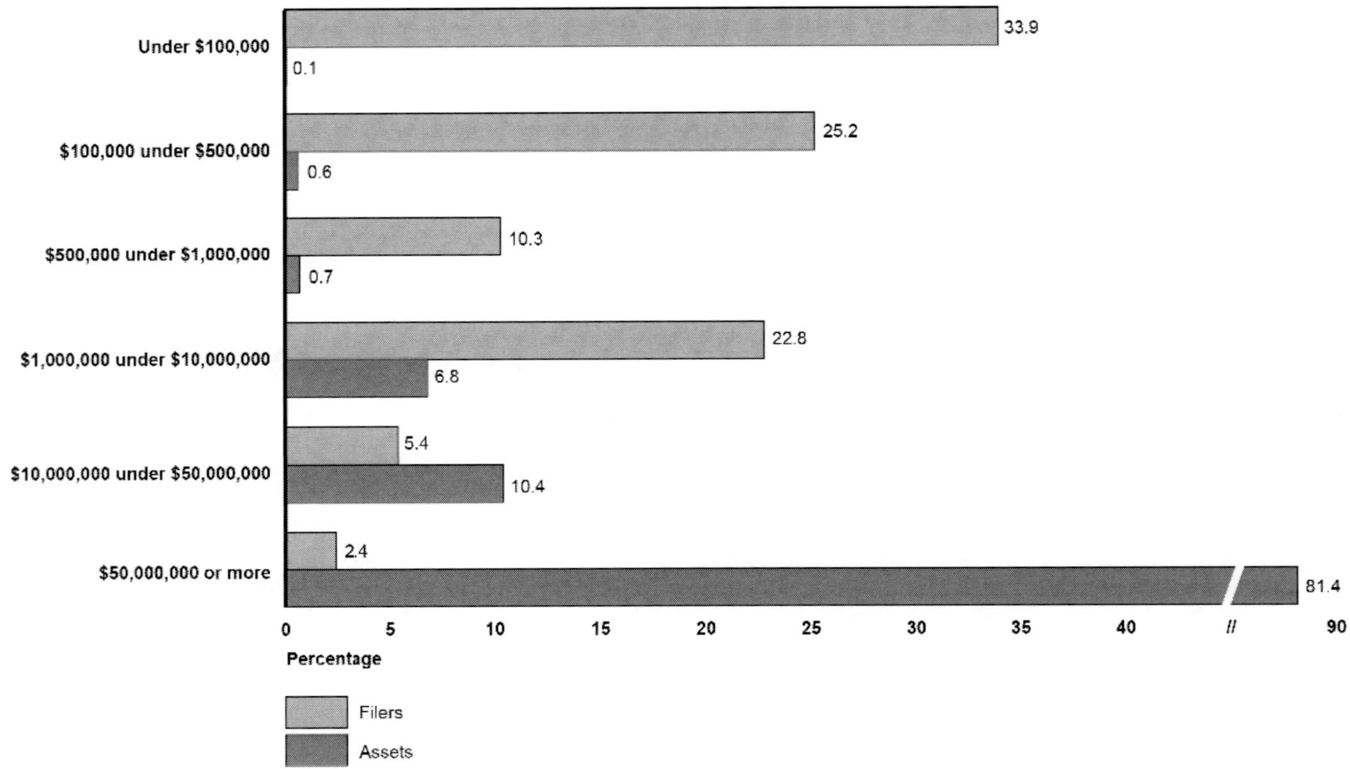

Source: GAO analysis of SOI data from Forms 990 and 990-EZ. | GAO-15-164.

Note: Statements about sampling errors are reported in appendix III.

Figure 4. Percentage of Charitable Organization Filers and Assets by Asset Category, Tax Year 2011.

The human services sector represents 38 percent of the total population of charitable organizations that file Form 990 or 990-EZ returns, followed by the education sector at 18 percent and the health sector at 13 percent. For more information by mission category, see appendix III. All three sectors cover a diverse range of programs and serve different segments of the population. The human services sector includes activities related to employment, housing and shelter, and youth development. Education includes elementary, secondary, vocational, and technical schools and universities. Health includes hospitals, mental health and crisis intervention, and medical research.

The assets of charitable organizations that file Forms 990 or 990-EZ returns are concentrated in the health and education sectors, which held about 75 percent of the total assets—more than $2 trillion—while the human services sector held almost $324 billion (or about 11 percent) of the total. In addition to being concentrated in a few sectors, a large proportion of total assets were controlled by a relatively small number of charitable organizations. Of the charitable organizations that file a Form 990 or Form 990-EZ, less than 3 percent held more than 80 percent of the assets, as shown in figure 4.[25] These organizations were primarily from the health and education sectors. Over 59 percent of charitable organizations that file Forms 990 or 990-EZ returns (with less than $500,000 in assets) held less than 1 percent of all assets.

Most of the expenses of charitable organizations that filed Form 990 were for program services, which are mainly activities that further the organization's tax-exempt purposes. Total expenses of charitable organizations are broken down on the Form 990 into program service expenses, management and general expenses, and fundraising expenses.[26] About eighty-seven percent of Form 990 charitable organization expenses in 2011 were for program services, about 12 percent for general management, and about 1 percent for fundraising.

As we noted in our 2002 report, charitable organizations have discretion in determining how to charge and allocate expenses for program services, general management, and fundraising.[27] The differences in methods can result in charities with similar activities allocating expenses differently among expense categories. This complicates interpretation of these data. For more information on expenses, see appendix III.

EO Receives Indications of Noncompliance from a Variety of Sources, but Declining Resources Complicate Efforts to Effectively Oversee Charitable Organizations

EO Receives Indications of Noncompliance from a Variety of Sources

Through its examinations, IRS can analyze the operations and finances of tax-exempt organizations and propose tax assessments or changes to exempt status when necessary. In general, IRS attempts to select entities that it believes are likely to have violated requirements, such as unauthorized use of an organization's assets, or engaging in political activity. On the basis of these examinations, IRS can accept the Form 990 as filed or can change the status of the entity, impose excise taxes for certain types of violations, or revoke the tax-exempt status if the violations are serious enough. It can also assess taxes if an entity has not fully paid employment taxes or taxes on unrelated business income. IRS can also advise organizations on complying with the law in the future. This can include sending written advisories to organizations advising them of specific issues that need to be addressed.

IRS receives indications of noncompliance from a variety of sources that can lead to examinations, as shown in figure 5.

EO initiated 8,413 exams of tax-exempt organization returns in 2013 and 4,495 of these (or about 53 percent) were exams of charitable organizations. As shown in table 2, the largest source for these exams (41 percent) was the category that includes the IRS National Research Program project. EO participated in an IRS National Research Program project on employment taxes in 2013, which contributed to an unusually high number of exams during that year.

The next largest source (22 percent) was Form 990 data analytics. In 2008, IRS redesigned the Form 990 for the purposes of promoting compliance and increasing transparency. The redesigned form requires filing organizations to supply more in-depth information than previous versions. For example, the form includes new questions on governance, compensation, activities, relationships with related organizations, international activities, fundraising, non-cash contributions, and other compliance areas. A team of EO specialists developed data-mining queries (based on the redesigned form) to identify suspected inaccuracies or anomalies. For example, with the new Form 990, EO can search for whether an organization reports that it has a mortgage and receives rental income—suggesting that it has unrelated business income. If the organization does not file a Form 990-T, Exempt Organization Business Income Tax Return to report any unrelated business income, IRS is more likely to select the organization for examination. As of April 2014, EO had developed a list of over 150 condition codes based on return line entries to identify potential noncompliance issues.

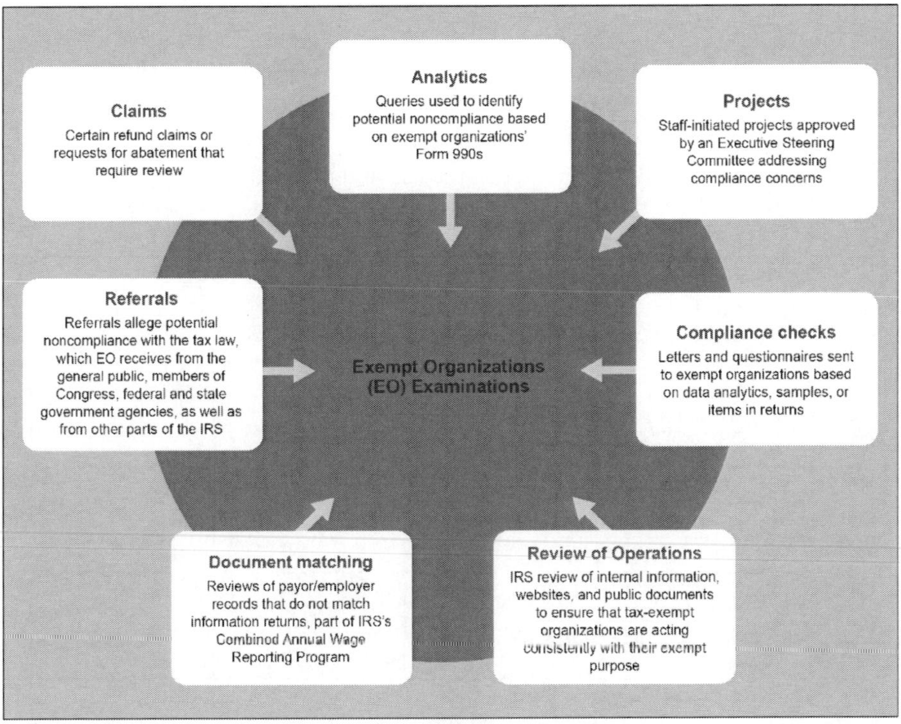

Figure 5. Sources of Charitable Organization Examinations in 2013.

Of the charitable organization examinations initiated in fiscal year 2013, 632 (or 14 percent) were the result of referrals (including news items)—communication EO receives from internal and external sources alleging potential noncompliance with the tax law. EO managers told us referrals are prioritized so that those involving a serious breach of public trust or abuse—such as financial investigations or allegations of terrorism—are to be examined right away. On the other hand, high profile referrals— referrals resulting from a media exposé or involving a well-known organization—are not necessarily high priority, and may not be examined right away. The two most common sources of referrals for all tax-exempt organizations in 2013 were the general public, with about 81 percent of the 6,940 total referrals, and other IRS functional areas, with about 12 percent of the total. The specific potential violations most commonly alleged were that income or assets were being used for private benefit, the organization was involved in a political campaign; or the organization failed to report employment, income, or excise tax liability properly.[28]

Table 2. Source of Charitable Organization Examinations Initiated, Fiscal Year 2013

Source	Number of examinations initiated	Percent of examinations initiated
IRS National Research Program project on employment taxes and other[a]	1,851	41.2
Form 990 data analytics	994	22.1
Document matching	444	9.9
Referral received from outside IRS	361	8.0
Referral received from inside IRS	255	5.7
Review of Operations	178	4.0
Refund claims or requests for abatement	145	3.2
Compliance checks – letters	131	2.9
Compliance checks – questionnaires	120	2.7
News items[b]	16	0.4
Total	4,495	100.0

Source: IRS's Return Inventory Classification System. | GAO-15-164

[a]Includes instances where a return was added during an examination—either the same return from a different year or a different return.

[b]Includes referrals IRS received in the form of submitted news clippings; does not include referrals received from members of the media, which IRS groups with referrals received from the general public.

Limited Resources Contribute to Fewer Examinations

With IRS budget cuts, the number of EO FTEs has declined over the past several years, leading to a steady decrease in the number of organizations examined. The total number of FTEs in the EO division decreased from 889 to

842 (about 5 percent) and the number of FTEs doing examinations declined from 529 to 493 (about 7 percent) between fiscal years 2010 and 2013, as shown in table 3.

Table 3. Number of FTEs in IRS Exempt Organization Division by Function, Fiscal Years 2010-2013

Fiscal year	Rulings and Agreements	Examinations[a]	Customer Education and Outreach	Director's Office/Program Management[b]	Total
2010	341	529	9	10	889
2011	328	534	12	12	886
2012	319	516	11	12	858
2013	326	493	11	12	842

Source: IRS officials. | GAO-15-164

[a]llot all employees perform examinations.

[b]Supports the Director, EO and all of EO's functional areas, tracks EO's budget, monitors hiring and promotions, measures and reports EO's performance and performance goals internally, and helps ensure that EO is responsive to the needs of the headquarters Tax-Exempt and Government Entities Division, and the Commissioner.

IRS examines only a small percentage of charitable organizations that file returns, including private foundations, as shown in table 4.[29] EO examination rates were lower, relative to other IRS divisions. For charitable organizations, the examination rate was about 0.7 percent in 2013, while for individual and corporate tax returns it was 1 percent and 1.4 percent, respectively.[30] A comparison of tables 3 and 4 also shows that the number of employees performing exams has declined while the number of returns filed has increased. From fiscal year 2011 to 2013, the exam rate decreased from .81 percent to .71 percent (by about 12 percent).

Table 4. Examination Rate of Charitable Organizations, Fiscal Years 2011-2013

Fiscal year	Returns filed in previous year	Returns examined in fiscal year	Examination rate
2011	725,888	5,888	0.81%
2012	753,985	5,864	0.78%
2013	763,149	5,426	0.71%

Source: IRS's Return Inventory Classification System and IRS officials. | GAO-15-164

As shown in table 5, examinations may result in no change to the amount of taxes owed or the tax-exempt status, the assessment of taxes or penalties, or the revocation of tax-exempt status. The no-change rate over the past three years has been between 30 and 34 percent. According to EO officials, IRS uses change and no-change rates as one indicator of how well it is targeting exams. Therefore higher no-change rates indicate that IRS is spending resources examining compliant entities. The 30 percent no-change rate for charitable organizations is relatively high when compared to the rate for some other filers. For example, in 2013, the no-change rate for all examinations of individual tax returns ranged from 9 to 12 percent, depending on the type of exam that was conducted.

Table 5. Number of Charitable Organization Examinations Closed and Results, Fiscal Years 2011- 2013

Fiscal year	Number of return closures	Percent of return closures with nochange[a]	Percent of return closures with written advisory	Percent of return closures with agreed tax or penalty	Percent of return closures with agreed termination[b]	Percent of return closures with revocation	Delinquent return secured/ related return secured	Other[c]	Total results
2011	5,888	30%	14%	15%	1%	4%	19%	16%	100%
2012	5,864	34%	11%	23%	1%	2%	18%	12%	100%
2013	5,426	30%	16%	27%	1%	3%	14%	10%	100%

Source: GAO Analysis of IRS data from IRS Return Inventory Classification System. | GAO-15-164.

Note: Percentages do not total to 100 due to rounding.

[a]Does not include written advisories, as those are considered a change.

[b]IRS cannot initiate the termination of an organization. Termination occurs when a tax-exempt organization notifies IRS that it has ended its operations, either through shutting down, transferring its assets, or merging with another tax-exempt organization.

[c]Includes results such as those unagreed by the taxpayer, or changes by IRS to a taxpayer's related return, such as a prior-year return.

An organization may be subject to a tax assessment or penalty charges for filing a late return, for failure to provide required document, or for late payment of taxes. IRS can also revoke tax-exempt status when charitable organizations (or individuals responsible for the organization) violate certain rules. The organization would have to reapply as a tax-exempt organization and start the process over. Revocations may result when an organization is found to be engaging in non-exempt activities, operating in a commercial manner, or allowing inurement of net earnings or assets of the organization to benefit an officer, director, or a key employee who has a personal or private interest in the activities of the organization. This type of enforcement action happens infrequently.

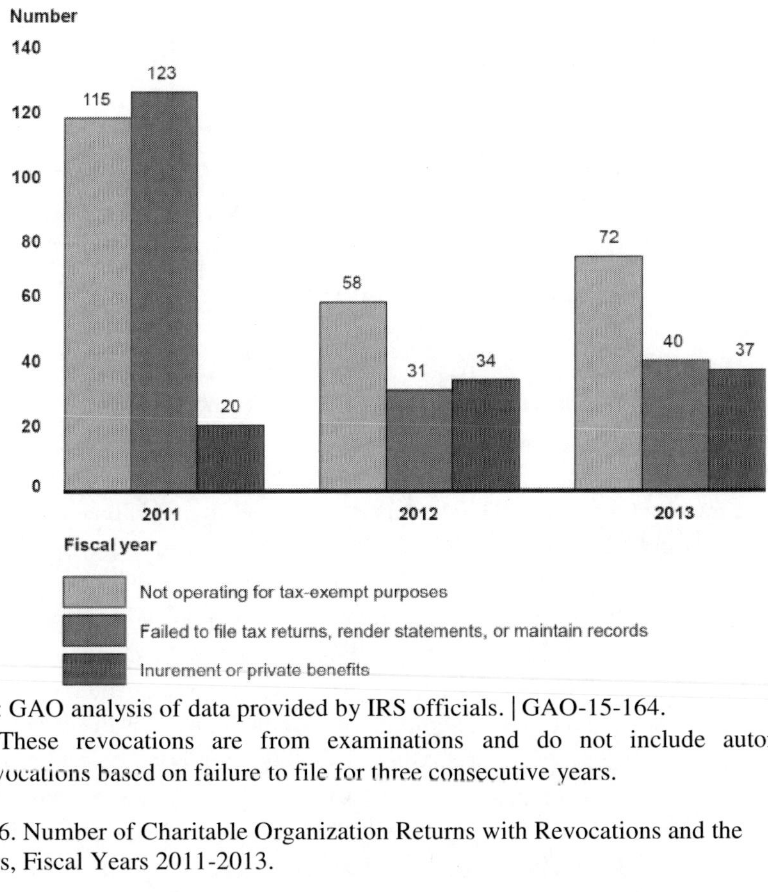

Source: GAO analysis of data provided by IRS officials. | GAO-15-164.
Note: These revocations are from examinations and do not include automatic revocations based on failure to file for three consecutive years.

Figure 6. Number of Charitable Organization Returns with Revocations and the Reasons, Fiscal Years 2011-2013.

An exam may also identify issues—such as a proposed expansion of an unrelated business income producing activity, or a failure to properly report required information, such as special fundraising activities or officer compensation. If enlarged, these issues could jeopardize the tax-exempt status of the organization. However, there is no change in the tax-exempt status of the organization. Instead, the examiner will issue a closing letter with a written advisory addendum to the organization identifying the noncompliance issues found during the examination which, if corrected, would bring the organization into compliance.

As figure 6 shows, the number of charitable organization returns with revocations declined from 2011 to 2013. Generally, the most often-cited reason for the revocation was that the charitable organization was not operating for a charitable purpose. The exception was in 2011, where the failure to file returns and other records was slightly higher. Operating for the benefit of private interests was another reason for a revocation.[31]

THE IMPACT OF EO COMPLIANCE EFFORTS ON CHARITABLE ORGANIZATIONS IS UNKNOWN, DUE TO LACK OF KEY PERFORMANCE MEASURES AND GOALS AND LACK OF COMPLETE DATA

The EO Business Division has faced challenges over the past several years from declining budgets and staffing and from the complexity and the sensitivity of their workload, which includes regulating the political activity of tax-exempt organizations. EO's ability to address these challenges has been hindered by a lack of performance measures that EO management could use to fully assess and communicate how effective their efforts have been. EO managers have introduced some timeliness measures that may lead to efficiency gains by helping them track their inventory of applications, referrals, and exam cases and identify bottlenecks as they occur. However, EO managers lack compliance goals and measures for assessing their progress in ensuring that charitable organizations are conforming to their charitable purpose and other aspects of the tax law. EO is developing a new approach to identify and select organizations for examination. EO also introduced a streamlined application form for smaller organizations seeking tax-exempt status that may reduce administrative burden. However, the limited amount of information that will be available about these organizations raises questions about how IRS will identify noncompliance issues for this particular segment of charitable organizations. In addition, a lack of timely, accurate digitized data from the Form 990 further complicates oversight efforts.

Lack of Quantitative, Results-Oriented Goals and Measures for Improving Compliance Limits Ability to Assess Effectiveness of EO Oversight

EO has developed measures and goals to track its output of application reviews and examinations, but these do not measure impact on compliance. EO managers develop an annual work plan, which lists the research projects and exams they plan to initiate over the course of the year. The work plan includes goals for the number of cases they plan to start and close within the year, and the estimated number of staff days for each project. EO management uses a quarterly dashboard to track their progress against the workload goals, as set forth in their annual work plan. However, these performance goals and measures do not show the impact of EO efforts on compliance. These are measures that are useful for monitoring processes within EO, but they do not measure outcomes— such as improvements in the compliance rate for the charitable organization sector. Developing outcome-oriented goals and establishing measures to assess the actual results of EO activities (compared to their intended purpose) can help EO improve performance and determine whether programs have produced desired results.

EO Examinations managers use the examination change rate as a measure of compliance. The change rate is measured as the percentage of exams that result in a written advisory, a change in the amount of taxes, penalties, or fines an organization owes, or a change in the organization's tax-exempt status. This change rate that EO reports from exams may be a useful indicator of how accurately EO is selecting charitable organizations for exam but it has limitations as a compliance measure. EO does not use a random sample of organizations to estimate the change rate for the charitable sector as a whole and—except in the case of certain projects described below—it does not estimate the rate by type of charitable organization or by compliance issue. Change rates based on nonrandom exam selection procedures cannot be used to enhance compliance by focusing enforcement efforts on areas with the highest risk of noncompliance. In addition, EO's change rate is ambiguous as a measure of compliance because while it includes the number of written advisories that EO managers send following an exam, EO managers do not track the percentage of organizations that received a written advisory in the past and continued to be noncompliant.[32]

In addition to lacking some key compliance measures, EO managers do not set specific, measurable goals related to improving the compliance levels of tax-exempt organizations, either as a whole or for charitable organizations in particular. One reason it is difficult to set compliance goals, according to IRS and EO officials, is that IRS has not completed a study for charitable organizations that establishes a compliance baseline. In order to track progress toward a compliance goal, generally-accepted evaluation standards require establishing a baseline for compliance measures and recording how these measures change over time.

A possible source for such a baseline is IRS's National Research Program (NRP) but the cost of establishing a baseline may be large. The NRP examines a sample of tax returns to estimate rates of noncompliance for all taxpayers and for different types of taxpayers and tax issues. According to IRS and Exempt Organizations officials, it would be useful to have a research program like the NRP identify compliance baselines for EO. More compliance data on the EO sector would allow EO examiners to better select organizations for exam and would potentially reduce the no-change rate. However, these officials also point out that such a project requires a considerable investment of resources. They also say undertaking such a large-scale long-term project may not be feasible, given the resource constraints faced by IRS.

Another possible source of baseline data is the projects initiated by the EO Examinations Unit. EO Examinations sponsors new research projects each year to help identify non-compliance (which can include estimating a change rate) by types of operations, by segments of the charitable sector, or around a particular issue or item from the Form 990. A project can begin when EO decides that potential for noncompliance exists for a certain issue based on data analytic queries, referrals, or some other source (as described above). A random sample of organizations in that segment is selected for review. EO managers said they generally judge a project to be successful if it achieves a change rate of 80 percent or higher. For example, if 80 percent or more of the returns examined as part of the review result in a change in the amount of taxes, penalties, or fines the organization owes, a change in the organization's tax-exempt status, or a significant change in the organization's operations, EO managers may then decide to incorporate the original query as part of their regular examination selection criteria.

However, EO does not use the results of the projects as baselines to assess whether the strategies adopted as a result of the projects have improved compliance among the segments of the tax-exempt sector that were studied in the projects. EO managers see these projects as a way to gather information they can use to develop strategies to address emerging issues, measure overall levels of compliance, and address areas of known non-compliance. But the impact on compliance remains unclear, because EO does not consistently follow up to measure the project impact in subsequent years or policy changes made as a result of the project. Even when a full research project using a representative sample is not justified given EO's resource limitations, other approaches may still provide useful information about compliance. For example, tracking the frequency in exams of issues that were identified in the project, while not an adequate compliance measure due to the nonrandom exam selection procedures, could provide insight into whether the issues are still a reason for concern.

An example of how establishing a baseline could have helped EO measure the effect on compliance of policy changes is EO's project that reviewed charitable organizations providing consumer credit counseling. The project examined over 200 organizations and IRS revoked, terminated, or proposed revoking the exemptions of around 60 percent of these organizations for abuses such as failure to provide education, operating as a commercial business, or serving the private interest of directors, officers, and related entities. According to the 2011 Exempt Organizations Annual Report, this project helped to stimulate legislative changes in 2006, including new tax rules governing exempt credit counseling organizations.[33]

However, IRS has not evaluated the effect of changes in the law that came about as a result of the project on subsequent compliance by charitable organizations that provide credit counseling. Because the project examined over 200 of the credit counseling organizations, including the 63 largest, it may have had sufficient coverage of this part of the charitable sector to provide a baseline for assessing the effect of the legislative changes on compliance. According to EO officials, they decided not to open a large volume of new credit counseling cases after the initial project was completed because the initial project still had cases in the appeals process and the relevant sections of the 2006 legislation had phase-in provisions under which the provision took full effect for tax years after January 1, 2011. However, EO currently has no plans to undertake such a study in the future.

EO officials told us that they intend to change their source-based approach to selecting and conducting exams starting in 2015, in order to make better use of limited resources. They said they intend to rely more on data mining queries based on the redesigned Form 990 to detect high-risk areas of noncompliance and to prioritize enforcement efforts. This approach may also better conform to strategies IRS lays out in their strategic plan for 2014-2017, which calls for IRS to develop improved research-driven methods and tools to detect and combat noncompliance and improve resource allocation.[34] As an example, EO officials also report they will prioritize case selection according to criteria that give more weight to more consequential outcomes. A data mining query generating a lot of revocations would take priority over a query that may only generate written advisories. They hope their new approach will allow them to better select cases for exam and to measure their effectiveness. However, this new approach is still in early stages of development and they are starting to implement it in FY 2015. Also, without compliance goals, related performance measures, and more complete indicators of compliance, it will be difficult to assess the effectiveness of the new strategy.

Developing measures of compliance and determining the impact of projects and exams on compliance is challenging. As we've discussed in past reports, IRS researchers have found it difficult to determine the extent to which its enforcement actions deter noncompliance or its services improve compliance among taxpayers who want to comply.[35] The challenges to determining impact include collecting reliable compliance data, developing reasonable assumptions about taxpayer behavior, and accounting for factors outside of IRS's actions that can affect taxpayer compliance, such as changes in the tax law. Nevertheless, even if IRS (or in this case, EO) is unable to empirically estimate the extent to which its actions directly affected compliance rates, periodic measurements of compliance levels can indicate the extent to which compliance is improving or declining and can provide a basis for reexamining existing programs and triggering corrective actions, if necessary.

Best practices indicate that establishing results-oriented goals can help agency officials demonstrate they have thought through how the activities and initiatives they are undertaking are likely to lead to meaningful results in line with programmatic goals. An example of a results-oriented goal for EO would be a specific, measurable increase in compliance rates for particular types of organizations (such as for the credit counseling organizations described above) or for certain issues that have been problematic in the past (such as failure to pay employment taxes). We have also previously reported that setting results-oriented goals, establishing performance measures and related performance indicators with targets in meeting such goals, and reporting on progress against those goals are the hallmarks of effective management.[36] The absence of results-oriented goals and related performance measures for compliance does not allow EO officials to compare the success of different initiatives against one another, determine whether their compliance strategy is working as intended, or allocate resources to those activities that have the most impact on compliance levels.

New Streamlined Application and Review Process Raises Questions about Whether IRS Will Collect Adequate Information to Indentify Noncompliance among Smaller-Sized Organizations

In May 2013, Treasury Inspector General for Tax Administration (TIGTA) found that applicants for tax-exempt status experienced significant delays in the review of their applications.[37] Specifically, it reported that as of December 2012, many organizations had not received an approval or denial letter—more than two years after they submitted their applications. TIGTA also reported that the EO Rulings & Agreements function did not have specific timeliness goals for processing applications, such as potential political cases, that require significant follow-up with the organizations. The Taxpayer Advocate also reviewed EO operations and concluded that EO management did not have meaningful performance measures required for effective management oversight of the application process such as how long it takes, on average, to process applications that cannot be disposed of during initial screening and what percentage of inventory had not been reviewed in nine months or more.[38]

The lack of meaningful performance measures compounded other challenges faced by EO management. As discussed earlier, the number of charitable organizations recognized as tax-exempt by IRS increased over the past decade, as the number of employees has declined along with budget cuts. In addition, the auto-revocation process that began in 2011 (following changes to legislation in 2006) inadvertently led to an increase in the number of applications. By revoking the status of organizations that had not filed in three years, the process revoked the status of hundreds of thousands of organizations that no longer existed as intended, but also purged thousands of organizations that still merited tax-exempt status, but may have been unaware of their filing requirements. Once their status was automatically revoked, many applied for reinstatement, leading to a spike in applications. According to IRS senior officials, other challenges faced by EO management included outdated information technology records management systems, making it difficult for managers to understand and manage the size of the application backlog.

EO managers introduced performance measures and goals to help address these challenges and the concerns about applications inventory raised by TIGTA and the Taxpayer Advocate. For fiscal years 2013 and 2014, EO managers set a goal to eliminate the backlog of applications waiting for review for 270 days or more. To assess their progress in managing the inventory of applications, EO managers focused on performance measures such as number of applications received and closed, average age of applications inventory, and number of cases still pending after 270 days. They anticipate that these measures will allow them (for the first time) to track their progress, to more readily identify choke points and the reasons why slowdowns are occurring, and to react accordingly. Managers can now access this information through a weekly dashboard to monitor the inventory and communicate to senior EO management on a quarterly basis. As of September 2014, IRS Exempt Organizations officials reported they had closed over 117,000 cases in FY 2014, an increase of 121 percent over the prior year's closings. They also reported that the end of year inventory was 22,759, as compared to 65,718 at the end of FY 2013.

EO managers also introduced a streamlined application review process to reduce their inventory of aged cases. Initially, application reviewers relied more heavily on attestation statements made under penalty of perjury, rather than with substantiating documents. For example, if an organization failed to include a narrative statement describing its activities as required by the application Form 1023, IRS would ask the organization to attest that it met the operational test for tax-exempt status, rather than hold the case open until the organization submitted the appropriate paperwork.[39] Similarly, applicants that failed to submit organizing documents—which are important because they describe how the organization's purpose and assets comply with tax-exempt purposes set forth in section 501(c)(3)—would need to attest that they had the appropriate organizing documents and that they met statutory and regulatory requirements, rather than provide actual documents. EO officials said attestation statements allowed applicants to indicate that they were fully aware of the application requirements, but they were not used in isolation. For example, if an application indicated the possibility of private inurnment, the reviewer was supposed to ask the applicant about this issue and would not rely solely on attestation. In the spring of 2014, EO managers determined the interim guidance for application reviewers was unclear, and they told reviewers there must be a narrative and organizing documents, although the IRM has not yet been updated to reflect this change. The new, streamlined procedures initially applied only to cases in the applications inventory that were more than a year old, but were extended in May, 2014 to all existing inventory. EO officials told us these streamlined review procedures are temporary and they are commissioning a study to evaluate their effectiveness and efficiency.

In addition, in July 2014, EO managers introduced a new application form for relatively small organizations. This application adopts the same approach of substituting attestation for documentation as used initially in the streamlined inventory procedure. The new application (Form 1023- EZ) can be used by certain organizations with annual gross receipts of $50,000 or less and assets of $250,000 or less seeking tax-exempt status.[40] This form is considerably shorter than Form 1023 (3 pages compared to 12 pages), asks fewer questions, and the questions are primarily yes/no questions or checking a box for attestation.[41] Form 1023- EZ does not require detailed information, such as organization documents, financial statements, or explanations, descriptions, or narratives about activities, as is required on Form 1023. EO managers anticipate that the majority of new applicants will use the streamlined Form 1023-EZ.

Several organizations, including the National Council of Nonprofits and National Association of State Charity Officials (NASCO) have raised concerns about the impact of the shorter application Form 1023-EZ on compliance. These concerns include decreasing the quality of information the IRS needs to make informed decisions about granting tax-exempt status, making it easier for "scam" charities to obtain tax-exempt status, and shifting IRS oversight obligations onto the public, the funding community, and state charity regulators. Likewise, the Taxpayer Advocate also raised concerns about the streamlined 1023-EZ form, including a lack of empirical data demonstrating that organizations anticipating less than $50,000 in gross annual receipts pose low risks to compliance, a failure to conduct a comprehensive evaluation of downstream consequences of the streamlined application, and a post-implementation evaluation plan that relies on the limited effect of a small number of audits to correct potential compliance problems. EO officials told us they disagreed with the Taxpayer Advocate's findings.

EO officials said that they conducted a risk assessment of their new streamlined application process. As part of the risk assessment, IRS identified several compliance-related risks, including the possibility of an increase in fraudulent applications and consequent potential loss of revenue, due to tax deductible contributions to organizations that were not eligible for exemption. To address these compliance risks, the IRS risk assessment cited the need for a more robust back-end review of newly-exempt organizations that had received their status through the streamlined process. This would include increased use of quality control checks, audits, and other reviews, and an enhanced EO Examination process to identify ineligible organizations.

EO managers intend to review a sample of organizations that used the Form 1023-EZ to apply for tax exempt status to learn about the population of organizations applying for exemption using the new, shorter form, including their eligibility to use the form. This phase started in July 2014 (when the new form was introduced to the public), and occurs after an organization submits an application and before IRS makes a determination on tax-exempt status. IRS plans to review a random sample of 3 percent—an estimated 1,260—of applications submitted using the new streamlined 1023-EZ form. According to EO officials, this sample size was based on a reliability factor and was then adjusted based on staffing resource capacity.[42] As part of determining eligibility to use the shorter form, the reviewers are supposed to request from the filers in the sample such items as a detailed description of past, present, and future activities, and revenues and expenses for the most recently completed year.

The EO Examinations function will also conduct post-determination (i.e., after tax exempt status has been determined) compliance reviews of organizations that applied for and received their tax-exempt status through the streamlined application review as well as organizations that applied for and received their tax-exempt status using the shorter Form1023-EZ. The compliance reviews of the first group—organizations that received their tax-exempt status through the streamlined review process—will begin during FY 2015. For this review, EO plans to select a random sample of exempt organizations reviewed under the streamlined process to provide information about the subsequent compliance characteristics of organizations that received their status in this way. EO recently approved guidance for reviewing these returns, which lists potential areas of noncompliance, such as legislative or overseas activities, compensation issues, and unrelated business activity.

According to Tax-Exempt and Government Entities Division and EO officials, post-determination compliance reviews of organizations that used the Form 1023-EZ to apply for tax-exempt status will begin in late FY 2015 or early FY 2016. For this review, EO plans to take a random sample of exempt organizations that filed the Form 1023-EZ to provide information about the subsequent compliance characteristics of organizations that filed the shorter form. They anticipate they will use the same review procedures for the Form 1023-EZ exams as they use for the streamlined review process. However, they also report some modifications will be necessary due to the limited information on the EZ application itself as well as the fact that eligible organizations would typically be filing the Form 990-N as opposed to the more detailed Form 990 or even Form 990-EZ. The limited amount of information that will be available about these organizations because of the shorter application form and information return raises questions about how IRS will identify noncompliance issues for this particular segment of charitable organizations.

Lack of Timely and Complete Data Limits IRS Ability to Provide Adequate Oversight of Charitable Organizations and to Provide for the Transparency of the Tax-Exempt Sector

The e-filing rate for tax-exempt organizations is significantly lower than for other taxpayers and organizations. In 2013, 38 percent of Forms 990, 990-EZ, and 990-PF were filed electronically, while in 2011, 64 percent of partnerships and 66 percent of S Corporations filed electronically.[43] The lower rate is due in large part to current law, requiring only very small and very large tax-exempt organizations to file electronically.[44] Larger tax-exempt organizations (those that that file at least 250 returns during the calendar year) are required to file electronically and smaller organizations (those that are excused from filing Form 990 or Form 990-EZ, generally because their gross receipts are normally less than $50,000 annually), must file an annual notice (Form 990-N) in electronic format. Medium-sized organizations—those too big to file the Form 990-N, but not big enough to file 250 returns—are not required to file electronically.

This lower rate means that there is less digitized data available for data mining and analytics and that IRS will have higher labor costs. IRS officials said that having more return information available electronically might improve examination selection. For instance, when IRS examination specialists suggested filters for an EO project to use in identifying potentially noncompliant issues, the lack of available electronic data prevented EO from using all of the filters. Further, IRS officials estimate that mandated electronic filing would save EO more than an estimated $1 million in labor costs over a three year period, although a complete study has not been performed.

In the FY 2015 Budget proposal, the administration proposed that Congress expand e-filing for tax-exempt organizations.[45] Expanded e-filing may result in more accurate and complete data becoming available in a timelier manner, which in turn, would allow IRS to more easily identify areas of noncompliance. In our 2014 report on partnerships and S corporations, we recommended that Congress consider expanding the mandate for partnerships and corporations to electronically file their tax returns in order to cover a greater share of filed returns.[46] We concluded that increased e-filing would increase the amount of digitized data available to IRS, which examiners could then use to identify which partnership and S corporation tax returns could be most productive to examine. Since many charitable organizations are organized as not-forprofit corporations, the same mandate could also cover 501(c)(3) charitable organizations.

Any option for an e-filing mandate would impose some burden on some tax return filers if (for example) they do not already possess the e-filing technology and they need to get access to it. However, expanded e-filing could also reduce taxpayer burden, since greater accuracy would reduce false-positives, allowing IRS to identify “bad actors” rather than organizations who made mistakes on their returns. In addition, the burden could be mitigated. The 2015 budget proposal would allow transition relief for up to three additional years after the date of enactment to begin electronic filing, for smaller organizations and organizations for which electronic filing would be an undue hardship without additional transition time.

According to IRS, electronic filing also increases transparency for the tax-exempt community because more searchable data becomes publicly available faster than paper-filed returns, which must first be converted to machine readable format. Once publicly available, the Form 990 data may be used by donors to make more informed contribution decisions and by researchers, analysts, and entrepreneurs to understand the tax-exempt sector better and to create information tools and services to meet the needs of the sector. Having Form 990 series return data faster would also be useful to state and local regulators, charity watch-dog groups, charitable beneficiaries, and the press. In addition, e-filing would allow the IRS to process returns more quickly and at a lower cost than when paper returns are filed. Representatives from across the nonprofit and law enforcement community with whom we spoke support this reform as a strategy for improving transparency and accountability.

Uncertainty about How Taxpayer Data Can Be Shared and Used Limits Collaboration between IRS and State Charity Regulators

To oversee charitable organizations, IRS collaborates with different federal and state entities, including DOJ and state charity regulators. IRS and DOJ officials identified no obstacles that prevent their collaboration for the enforcement of tax laws. IRS refers cases involving possible criminal matters to the DOJ Tax Division for investigation and possible prosecution. According to DOJ officials, the review and referral process is designed to maintain a separation between IRS and DOJ decision making to avoid the appearance of (or actual) abuse of executive power. As such, DOJ attorneys have little involvement with the IRS review and referral process. Once a case is referred to DOJ, prosecutors have access to the taxpayer information under IRC section 6103(h)(2).[47] DOJ Tax Division attorneys said they are familiar with the information-sharing framework under this IRC provision. This framework allows prosecutors access to the information they need to build a case.

However, state regulators and other subject matter specialists said statutory requirements for safeguarding taxpayer information and uncertainty about how these safeguards must be implemented limit state regulators' ability to use relevant information shared by IRS. They add that this may reduce regulators' ability to use that information to build cases against charitable organizations engaged in fraudulent or other criminal activity.

Barriers to information sharing between IRS and state charity regulators have been a long-standing challenge. Before legislation passed in 2006, IRS was only permitted to disclose to state charity regulators information concerning final denials of applications for tax-exempt status, revocations of tax-exempt status, and final notices of deficiencies.[48] In 2002 and 2005, we reported that this limited data sharing hampered state charity officials' efforts to identify charities which are defrauding the public or otherwise operating improperly.[49] At the time, state charity regulators told us that the lack of details impeded their efforts to track individuals who tried to re-establish similar, suspicious operations in other states. We recommended IRS propose revised legislation that would allow IRS to share more data—such as information about ongoing and closed examinations of charities—as a way to help IRS and states better use limited resources and to allow the states to more quickly respond to noncompliance.

In 2006, the PPA was enacted with provisions to facilitate information-sharing between IRS and state charity regulators.[50] The PPA expanded the type of information state charity regulators can receive to include sensitive, confidential information, such as revenue agents' reports regarding proposed revocations and notices of deficiencies.[51] IRS can now share information about certain proposed revocations and proposed denials before an administrative appeal is made and a final revocation or denial issued. In addition to the information IRS is now allowed to share with state charity regulators, IRS also makes revocations publicly available: IRS lists revocations in the Internal

Revenue Bulletin, although the reason for revocations resulting from exam are not given or made public.[52]

While the PPA expanded the types of information IRS could share with state charity regulators, the law also placed safeguards on that information. For the first time, the PPA subjected state charity regulators to the same criminal penalty provisions of the Internal Revenue Code that all other recipients of tax information are subject to, making it a criminal offense for any state official to willfully disclose information shared by the IRS under Section 6104(c) in a manner unauthorized by the Internal Revenue Code. To have access to the increased types of information now available, state charity regulators must sign a disclosure agreement with IRS in which they agree to certain safeguarding procedures for receiving and handling taxpayer data.

State charity regulators and other subject matter specialists we spoke with believe these safeguard requirements are unclear and difficult to implement. Although these requirements are the same as those that IRS and any state tax agencies receiving federal tax data must follow, most states do not have the resources, capacity, or infrastructure within their charitable oversight function to fulfill the requirements, according to subject matter experts with whom we spoke. For example, all disclosures provided by IRS must be reviewed by a state charity official, logged to record the receipt of the information, and stored behind at least two secured barriers, such as locked doors or cabinets. State charity regulators are also prohibited from entering the IRS shared data in a word processing program on a networked computer, unless lengthy security requirements are met.

Since the passage of the PPA, charity regulators in three states—California, New York, and Hawaii—signed a memorandum of understanding (MOU) with IRS to share information. However, despite the MOU, these state charity regulators still report challenges in storing and receiving data from IRS. A lack of clarity surrounding how they can use the data from IRS to build their own cases, and the criminal penalties attached to improper disclosure of the data, have prevented state charity regulators from incorporating IRS data into their investigations. For example, state charity regulators said when they learn that IRS is examining a charity located in their state for violating federal tax law, they must first contact the charity and request the documents it has already turned over to IRS. However, if the charity refuses or denies it has the requested documents, the state charity regulators do not believe they can enforce their request by citing the information provided to them by IRS. As a result, they seek to independently verify the information from the IRS (to the extent they are available) through other sources (such as the internet or the state registration database) before contacting the charity.

Also, according to subject matter experts, IRS interpretation of these rules has been inconsistent. As a result, regulators are unsure whether they are in violation of the safeguards requirements. According to state charity regulators, other states have not entered into information-sharing agreements with IRS because they view the safeguard requirements as overly burdensome, given their limited resources.

NASCO and the National Association of Attorneys General (NAAG) representatives credit IRS with trying to educate state regulators about the PPA requirements. IRS staff has given presentations at joint NAAG and NASCO conferences. According to the ACT 2013 report on exempt organizations, the IRS's designated EO federal/state liaison has worked to educate participating state agencies in the mechanics of PPA participation, has assisted with the safeguard procedure, and has linked state officials with appropriate IRS officials conversant in necessary information technology and security issues.[53] The report also credited IRS with initiating discussions with state charity regulators through a task force to develop a pragmatic approach for taking advantage of what is presently available under the PPA. IRS officials are also working on a new MOU that will clarify how state charity regulators can communicate to charities to let them know they have received information about them from IRS. In addition, to facilitate information sharing between IRS and state charity regulators, Treasury officials are in the process of reviewing the PPA and Congress's intent in drafting this legislation to determine whether additional flexibilities exist.

Despite these education and outreach efforts, state charity regulators are still unclear about how they are permitted to use IRS information to identify organizations violating state law and to build cases against them. The types of information PPA makes available would bolster state oversight efforts in a variety of ways. For example, according to the ACT report, state receipt of the names of organizations applying for exempt status would help states monitor startup entities that cease operations before the IRS responds to their for 1023 applications. EO officials told us that there are efforts underway to reduce processing times that should address this particular concern. Also according to the ACT report, state receipt of information about tax-exempt organizations receiving a proposed revocation of exemption would raise immediate questions about whether those organizations' assets are being properly applied to charitable purposes as required by state law.

The challenges to information sharing between IRS and state charity regulators are related to uncertainty about what is permissible under the PPA. With limited access to IRS information, state charity regulators do not always know why a charity has had its tax-exempt status revoked, if it is under examination, or if it has been fined, but maintains its tax-exempt status. The lack of information impedes state charity regulators' ability to identify and prosecute bad actors for violating state laws and hinders states' ability to inform donors of scam charities.

CONCLUSION

EO oversight of charitable organizations helps ensure that these entities abide by the purposes that justify their tax exemption and protects the sector from potential abuses and loss of confidence by the donor community. Over the past several years, reviewers have found that various units within the EO division could not fully assess or communicate their effectiveness because they lacked meaningful performance measures. EO managers have taken actions to address this deficiency by adding performance measures to help them track their inventory of applications, referrals, and exam cases and to ensure a level of quality assurance. EO has also developed its data analytics capacity to assist in selecting organizations for exam with greater audit potential. It has used these techniques and other information sources to select returns for examination and in some cases, has used the results of these exams to more systematically review certain tax issues. However, these actions have not addressed measuring the outcomes of EO activities (such as the effect of EO's actions on the compliance rate for the charitable sector as a whole), for specific segments of the sector (such as universities and hospitals), or for particular aspects of noncompliance (such as personal inurement or political activity). EO does not have the compliance measures or the quantitative, results-oriented compliance goals needed to assess its effect on the compliance of charitable organizations in any of these areas. Because EO does not measure the current level of compliance, it cannot set goals for increasing compliance or know to what extent its actions are affecting compliance.

The Exempt Organizations Business Division is grappling with several other challenges that complicate oversight efforts. The e-filing rate for tax-exempt organizations is significantly lower than for other taxpayers. This lower rate means that there is less digitized data available for data mining and analytics and higher labor costs for IRS. Expanded e-filing may result in more accurate and complete data becoming available in a timelier manner; in turn this would allow IRS to more easily identify areas of noncompliance. This legislative reform would also be useful to state and local regulators, charity watch-dog groups, charitable beneficiaries, and the press as a strategy for improving transparency and accountability.

A lack of clarity about how state charity regulators can use IRS data to build cases against suspect charitable organizations impedes regulators' ability to leverage IRS's examination work. IRS and Treasury officials are reviewing the statutory protections of taxpayer data and whether there is flexibility in regard to how state regulators must protect and can use federal tax data. IRS officials are also working on a new MOU that will clarify how state charity regulators can communicate to charities about information they have received from IRS. Once completed, these actions have the potential to enable greater collaboration between IRS and state charity regulators.

IRS budget and staffing levels have declined significantly over recent years. Officials and stakeholders we spoke to noted that IRS resources dedicated to EO oversight have not kept pace with growth in the sector and with the complexity of issues related to tax-exempt organizations. IRS faces difficult decisions about how to allocate resources dedicated to tax-exempt sector oversight and about what specific compliance issues to audit. IRS has already made trade-offs—such as examining fewer organizations and streamlining the application process for organizations seeking tax-exempt status—which may lead to some efficiencies, but will also result in less available information about these organizations. If IRS does not collect and use performance data to make sound decisions— especially given the likelihood of constrained budgets for the foreseeable future—the agency risks missing noncompliance, burdening tax-exempt organizations, and wasting scarce resources. Furthermore, it will be difficult for IRS to communicate agency progress to Congress and the public and thus, be held accountable.

MATTER FOR CONGRESSIONAL CONSIDERATION

Congress should consider expanding the mandate for 501(c)(3) organizations to electronically file their tax returns to cover a greater share of filed returns.

RECOMMENDATIONS

To improve oversight of charitable organizations, we recommend that the Commissioner of Internal Revenue take the following steps:

1) Direct EO to develop quantitative, results-oriented compliance goals and additional performance measures and indicators that can be used to assess impact of exams and other enforcement activities on compliance.
2) Continue to work with Treasury officials to do the following: review the flexibility afforded under PPA consistent with statutory protections of taxpayer data, clarify what flexibility state regulators have in how they protect and use federal tax data, make modifications to guidance, policies, or regulations as warranted, and clearly communicate this information with state charity regulators.

AGENCY COMMENTS AND OUR EVALUATION

We sent a draft of this report to the Commissioner of Internal Revenue and Assistant Attorney General for Administration, Department of Justice for comment. DOJ had no comments on our report. We received written comments from IRS's Deputy Commissioner for Services and Enforcement on December 4, 2014.

In its comments, IRS concurred with our recommendations and described ongoing and planned steps to 1) improve the application process for organizations seeking tax-exempt status and reduce the backlog of applications that had accrued in recent years, 2) refine its strategy and approach to better determine the effect of enforcement actions on compliance by tax-exempt organizations, including charitable organizations, and 3) improve the efficiency with which taxpayer information may be shared with state charity regulators through education efforts and outreach.

IRS also noted in its written comments that IRS's National Research Program (NRP) may not be well-suited for the tax-exempt sector, given the diversity that exists across the sector in regard to characteristics and compliance issues. Although we made no specific recommendation that EO be part of an NRP study, we note that the NRP has helped other IRS divisions determine compliance baselines and rates for types of taxpayers, such as corporations, where considerable diversity exits. While an NRP study could be a source for baseline data, we acknowledge that because of the high cost of such a study, it may not be practical at this time. Whatever approach to measuring compliance EO adopts, it should be consistent with our recommendation that EO develop quantitative, results-oriented compliance goals and additional performance measures that can be used to assess the impact of its activities on compliance.

We also received technical comments from IRS, which we incorporated into the final report where appropriate.

Sincerely yours,
James R. McTigue
Director, Tax Issues Strategic Issues Team

APPENDIX I: SCOPE AND METHODOLOGY

This report (1) describes what is known about the number, type, size, and other characteristics of 501(c)(3) charitable organizations; (2) describes IRS oversight activities for charitable organizations; (3) determines how IRS assesses its oversight efforts of charitable organizations to ensure they are meeting their charitable purposes; and (4) determines how IRS collaborates with state charity regulators and U.S. Attorneys to identify and prosecute organizations suspected of engaging in fraudulent or other criminal activity.

To address the first objective, we reviewed Internal Revenue Service (IRS) forms and publications. We also analyzed data from the IRS's Statistics of Income (SOI) files for Form 990, Return of Organization Exempt from Income Tax and Form 990-EZ Short Form, Return of Organization Exempt from Income Tax for tax year 2011 (the most recent year available). Although private foundations are considered charitable organizations, we did not analyze data from Form 990-PF, Return of Private Foundation or Form 990-N, e-Postcard because the data for these organizations is less complete and has other limitations. These limitations included total expenses not broken out into program service, management and general, and fundraising expenses; and private foundations not identified by mission category. In addition, our data excludes certain religious organizations, which qualify as 501(c)(3) organizations, but are not required to file a return. We also did not report data from prior years for the Form 990 and 990-EZ filers since the reporting threshold for organizations filing these returns varied from year to year, which makes year-to-year comparisons of the data difficult. These SOI samples were based on returns as filed, and did not reflect IRS audit results. Using SOI sampling weights, we estimated sampling errors for our estimates, which are reported in appendix III. Statements of difference are statistically significant.

SOI is a data set widely used for research purposes. SOI data on tax-exempt organizations are available to the public on the IRS website (http://www.irs.gov). IRS performs a number of quality control steps to verify the internal consistency of SOI sample data. For example, it performs computerized tests to verify the relationships between values on the returns selected as part of the SOI sample, and manually edits data items to correct for problems, such as missing items. We conducted several reliability tests to ensure that the data excerpts we used for this report were complete and accurate. For example, we electronically tested the data and used published data as a comparison to ensure that the data set was complete. To ensure accuracy, we reviewed related documentation and electronically tested for obvious errors. We concluded that the data were sufficiently reliable for the purposes of this report.

For the second objective, we reviewed IRS documentation and interviewed Exempt Organization (EO) officials on IRS oversight activities, such as the examination and revocation of charitable organizations. We also obtained data from IRS's Return Inventory Classification System (RICS) on examinations and results for fiscal years 2011 through 2013. Based on our review of documentation and interviews, we determined that this data was reliable for the purposes of this report. We also obtained data from IRS's Referral database on referrals received on charitable organizations and all tax-exempt organizations for fiscal years 2011 through 2013. Although we received referral data on charitable organizations, we did not use the data because we found it was not reliable for the purposes of this report. According to EO officials, reviewers were encouraged but not required to enter the organization's subsection category (i.e., that it was a 501(c)(3) charitable organization) into the referrals data base .The EO officials said that if the referral was found to have "no issue" by the reviewer, it may not have been assigned a subcategory because the subcategory was not required and it would be viewed (in this case) as not useful. Therefore, data on the number of referrals received, the source of referrals, and the type of referral violations that we received could have been undercounted if the data had been used. Although we did not use charitable organization referral data, we did use referral data on all tax-exempt organizations, as we found that data was reliable for the purposes of this report.

For the third objective, we reviewed relevant strategic and performance documents such as the annual reports and work plans, quarterly performance reports, and project summary reports. We interviewed IRS planning officials and division managers to determine the extent to which managers overseeing the tax-exempt sector set performance goals; develop measures to monitor their progress toward meeting goals; and use data to identify challenges, the cause of those challenges, and develop strategies to address those challenges. We reviewed past recommendations made by the Treasury Inspector General for Tax Administration (TIGTA) and National Taxpayer Advocate related to performance management and interviewed IRS managers about how they addressed the issues discussed in those reports. For criteria, we compared IRS information on performance measures and decision-making to *Standards for Internal Control in the Federal Government* and federal guidance on performance management.[1] We also applied the criteria concerning the administration, compliance burden and transparency that characterize a good tax system, as developed in our guide for evaluating tax reform proposals.[2] We also reviewed IRS plans to streamline the application process through the introduction of Form 1023EZ. We interviewed EO officials on how they plan to assess the impact of the new streamlined process on oversight efforts and reviewed available evaluation plans. We applied criteria from our 2012 guide on designing evaluations.[3]

To determine how IRS collaborates with state charity regulators and U.S. Attorneys, we reviewed various IRS documents, such as policy manuals, guidance, and memoranda of understanding. We also interviewed officials from IRS , U.S. Department of Justice (DOJ), and the National Association of State Charity Officials. For criteria, we identified different approaches for sharing information and collaboration based on our audit findings, as well as our past recommendations and recommendations made by the Advisory Committee on Tax Exempt and Government Entities.[4]

To provide additional context for all three objectives, we interviewed IRS officials, DOJ officials, state charity regulators, subject matter specialists, and stakeholder groups representing different types of exempt-organizations and private watchdog organizations that oversee charities about the adequacy of IRS oversight of charitable organizations; the challenges IRS faces providing effective oversight; and strategies to address those challenges.

APPENDIX II: TAX BENEFITS AND REQUIREMENTS FOR DIFFERENT TYPES OF TAX EXEMPT ORGANIZATIONS

The federal tax code provides a variety of tax benefits to organizations often referred to as "tax exempt." The exact nature of those benefits varies depending on the nature of the organization. Section 501 provides an exemption from federal income tax for the broadest range of organizations.[1] In addition to section 501, there are various other scattered provisions which give a full or partial tax exemption to certain specific types of entities and income.[2] This appendix focuses on organizations qualifying for a tax exemption under section 501, which will be referred to as tax exempt organizations. Within section 501, there is a division between charitable organizations, also known as 501(c)(3) organizations (after the subsection in which they are defined), and all other organizations qualifying for an exemption under section 501. The organizations that qualify for an exemption under section 501 but are not charitable organizations have been referred to as mutual benefit organizations or non-charitable nonprofits. Charitable organizations are further divided between those that are private foundations and all other charitable organizations, and private foundations are divided between operating and non-operating foundations. Each of these types of tax exempt organization—(1) mutual benefit organization, (2) charitable organization, (3) operating private foundation, and (4) non-operating private foundation—are subject to different requirements and receive different tax benefits.

Tax exempt organizations of all types are prohibited from engaging in certain transactions with the creator of an organization, a person who made a substantial contribution to the organization, a member of the family of the creator or substantial contributor, or a corporation controlled by a creator or substantial contributor.[3] Additionally, an organization operated for the primary purpose of carrying on a trade or business for profit is not exempt, on the grounds that all of its profits are payable to an exempt organization.[4] These restrictions apply to all types of tax exempt organizations. Certain types of mutual benefit organizations and all charitable organizations are also subject to the restriction that no part of their net earnings inures to the benefit of any private shareholder or individual. Additionally, a tax is imposed on income from any trade or business unrelated to the exercise or performance of the organization's exempt purpose.[5]

Charitable organizations, a subset of tax exempt organizations meeting the definition in section 501(c)(3) are as follows:

> "Corporations, and any community chest, fund, or foundation, organized and operated exclusively for religious, charitable, scientific, testing for public safety, literary, or educational purposes, or to foster national or international amateur sports competition (but only if no part of its activities involve the provision of athletic facilities or equipment), or for the prevention of cruelty to children or animals, no part of the net earnings of which inures to the benefit of any private shareholder or individual, no substantial part of the activities of which is carrying on propaganda, or otherwise attempting, to influence legislation (except as otherwise provided [elsewhere]), and which does not participate in, or intervene in (including the publishing or distributing of statements), any political campaign on behalf of (or in opposition to) any candidate for public office."

As stated above, no part of a charitable organization's net earnings can inure to the benefit of any private shareholder or individual. Additionally they must satisfy two tests: the organizational test and the operational test. To pass the organizational test, an entity must be organized exclusively for one or more exempt purposes, meaning that the governing instrument (such as a trust instrument, articles of incorporation, or association charter) must limit the purposes of the organization to one or more exempt purposes and does not expressly empower the organization to engage in activities not in furtherance of an exempt purpose except to an insubstantial degree.[6] The operational test requires that organizations engage primarily in activities that accomplish one or more of the exempt purposes listed in statute.[7] In general, new organizations seeking charitable organization status must apply for a determination of exempt status.[8] Churches, their integrated auxiliaries, and conventions or associations of churches, as well as organizations with gross receipts of $5,000 or less and that are not private foundations do not need to apply.[9]

Organizations which meet all the requirements to be charitable organizations receive tax benefits beyond those available to mutual benefit organizations. Contributions of cash or property to charitable organizations are deductible by individuals and corporations for federal income tax purposes up to certain percentages of adjusted gross income.[10] Such contributions are also exempt for estate and gift tax purposes.[11] Charitable organizations are exempt from the federal unemployment tax[12] and the federal gambling tax on lotteries.[13] Additionally, charitable organizations are exempt from certain requirements related to establishing and maintaining retirement plans for employees.[14]

Within the category of charitable organizations are private foundations. When applying for charitable organization status, an applicant is presumed to be a private foundation unless it can demonstrate that it is not a private foundation.[15] A charitable organization is not a private foundation if it is a church or convention or associations of churches, an educational institution, a medical or hospital care provider, medical education or research provider, or a government unit. A charitable organization is also not a private foundation if it is broadly publicly supported, as defined in section 509, or is a supporting organization of a broadly publicly supported organization. Organizations organized and operated exclusively for testing for public safety are also not private foundations. Charitable organizations not meeting one of these definitions are private foundations.

Private foundations are subject to certain tax consequences which do not apply to other charitable organizations. A 2 percent excise tax is imposed on the net investment income of private foundations.[16] A private foundation is also subject to additional taxes if it engages in self-dealing, has excessive business holdings, makes investments which jeopardize its charitable purpose, or makes certain taxable expenditures.[17] Finally, private foundations are subject to additional reporting requirements.[18]

Additional taxes and restrictions are imposed on foundations which do not meet the definition of an operating foundation. A private foundation is an operating foundation if is uses at least 85 percent of its income directly for the active conduct of charitable activities rather than for grantmaking and meets either an asset test, endowment test, or support test.[19] Private foundations that are not operating foundations are generally subject to a tax of 30 percent of the amount of undistributed income.[20] The percentage limits on the deductibility of contributions to non-operating private foundations are lower than for other charitable organizations.[21]

Aside from charitable organizations, section 501 lists 28 other types of nonprofits, often referred to as mutual benefit organizations, and which include unions, civic leagues, chambers of commerce, credit unions, and veteran organizations, among many others. For a complete list of the organizations listed in section 501, including charitable organizations, see below. Qualified pension, profit-sharing, and stock bonus plans are also exempt under section 501.[22] Unlike charitable organizations, gifts to these mutual benefit organizations are not deductible. Mutual benefit organizations are not generally exempt from the federal unemployment tax or the gambling tax, and do not have the additional flexibility in establishing employee retirement plans that is allowed charitable organizations.

Types of Tax Exempt Organizations Listed in Section 501

- Corporations organized by Act of Congress; Central Liquidity Facility for Federal Credit Unions; Resolution Trust Corporation; Resolution Funding Corporation
- Title-holding corporations
- Charitable organizations, including public charities, private foundations, religious, charitable, scientific, testing for public safety, literary, or educational, fostering national or international amateur sports competition, prevention of cruelty to children or animals
- Civic leagues, social welfare organizations, local associations of employees dedicated to charitable, educational, or recreational purposes
- Labor unions, agricultural, or horticultural organizations
- Trade associations, professional football leagues
- Social and recreational clubs
- Fraternal benefit societies providing payment of certain benefits to members
- Voluntary employees' beneficiary associations providing payment of certain employee benefits
- Domestic fraternal societies whose net earnings are devoted to religious, charitable, scientific, literary, educational, and fraternal purposes, which do not provide benefits to members
- Teachers' retirement fund associations
- Benevolent life insurance associations, mutual ditch or irrigation companies, mutual or cooperative telephone, electric, or water companies
- Cemetery companies
- Credit unions
- Small mutual insurance companies
- Corporations to finance crop operations
- Supplemental unemployment benefit trusts
- Pre-June 25, 1959 trusts to fund pension benefits
- Veterans' groups
- Group legal service organizations
- Black lung benefit trusts
- Multi-employer pension plan trusts
- Armed Forces insurance organizations established before 1880

- Employee Retirement Income Security Act trusts for certain terminated plans
- Multi-parent holding companies
- State-sponsored, high-risk insurance organizations
- State-sponsored worker compensation reinsurance organizations
- National railroad retirement investment trust
- Co-op health insurance issuers

APPENDIX III: ADDITIONAL TABLES

The tables in this statistical appendix supplement those in the letter and provide population estimates for Statistics of Income (SOI) data. After each table, notes indicate the sampling errors. We are confident the true estimates would be within these percentage points in 95 out of every 100 samples. The tables are for charitable organizations that filed Forms 990 or 990-EZ. Private foundations that file Form 990-PF, small charitable organizations that file Form 990-N, and charitable organizations that do not file returns have been excluded from this analysis.

Table 6. Number of Charitable Organization Filers by Mission Category, Tax Year 2011

Mission category	Number of filers	Percent
Arts, culture, and humanities	27,107	9.9
Education	47,928	17.5
Environment and animals	11,763	4.3
Health	35,267	12.9
Human services	105,444	38.4
International and foreign affairs	5,744	2.1
Public and social benefit	24,718	9.0
Religion-related	15,628	5.7
Mutual and membership benefit	687	0.3
Total	274,287	100.0

Source: GAO analysis of SOI data from Forms 990 and 990-EZ. | GAO-15-164

Note: All percent estimates have 95 percent confidence intervals that are within +/- 2 percentage points of the estimate itself. We excluded a very small sample of unknown or unclassified charitable organization filers from our analysis. Therefore, the amounts may not equal the total due to this exclusion and to rounding.

Table 7. Reported Amounts of Assets, Revenues, and Expenses of Charitable Organizations by Mission Category, Tax Year 2011

Mission category	Number of filers	Total assets (in millions)	Percent	Total revenues (in millions)	Percent	Total expenses (in millions)	Percent
Arts, culture, and humanities	27,107	106,969	3.5	30,458	1.8	28,756	1.8
Education	47,928	1,023,648	33.8	317,196	19.2	297,691	19.1
Environment and animals	11,763	42,837	1.4	16,103	1.0	14,546	0.9
Health	35,267	1,238,533	40.9	947,494	57.5	902,599	57.9
Human services	105,444	323,735	10.7	216,322	13.1	209,273	13.4
International and foreign affairs	5,744	32,048	1.1	27,677	1.7	25,309	1.6
Public and social benefit	24,718	218,573	7.2	80,800	4.9	69,165	4.4
Religion-related	15,628	25,217	0.8	9,295	0.6	8,624	0.6
Mutual and membership benefit	687	18,557	0.6	2,462	0.1	2,339	0.2
Total	274,287	3,030,133	100.0	1,647,905	100.0	1,558,401	100.0

Source: GAO analysis of SOI data from Forms 990 and 990-EZ. | GAO-15-164

Note: All percent estimates have 95 percent confidence intervals that are within +/- 2 percentage points of the estimate itself. We excluded a very small sample of unknown or unclassified charitable organization filers from our analysis. Therefore, the amounts may not equal the total due to this exclusion and to rounding.

Table 8. Reported Amounts of Assets, Revenues, and Expenses of Charitable Organizations, Tax Year 2011

Asset size category	Number of filers	Percent	Amount of assets (in millions)	Percent	Amount of revenues (in millions)	Percent	Amount of expenses (in millions)	Percent
Under $100,000	92,880	33.9	3,533	0.1	16,454	1.0	16,188	1.0
$100,000 under $500,000	69,185	25.2	17,097	0.6	26,751	1.6	25,705	1.6
$500,000 under $1,000,000	28,376	10.3	20,766	0.7	20,063	1.2	19,704	1.3
$1,000,000 under $10,000,000	62,488	22.8	207,027	6.8	174,150	10.6	171,684	11.0
$10,000,000 under $50,000,000	14,713	5.4	315,174	10.4	209,785	12.7	201,379	12.9
$50,000,000 or more	6,645	2.4	2,466,537	81.4	1,200,702	72.9	1,123,740	72.1
Total	274,287	100.0	3,030,133	100.0	1,647,905	100.0	1,558,401	100.0

Source: GAO analysis of SOI data from Forms 990 and 990-EZ. | GAO-15-164.

Note: All percent estimates have 95 percent confidence intervals that are within +/- 2 percentage points of the estimate itself. Amounts may not equal the total due to rounding.

Table 9. Charitable Organization Expenses by Mission Category, Tax Year 2011

Mission category	Number of filers	Percent of filers	Total expenses (in millions)	Program service expenses (in millions)	Percent of total expenses	Management and general expenses (in millions)	Percent of total expenses	Fundraising expenses (in millions)	Percent of total expenses
Arts, culture, and humanities	15,307	8.1	27,747	22,145	79.8	4,078	14.7	1,524	5.5
Education	29,632	15.6	296,473	255,998	86.3	35,038	11.8	5,437	1.8
Environment and animals	8,407	4.4	14,231	11,921	83.8	1,549	10.9	761	5.3
Health	28,122	14.8	902,044	784,358	87.0	114,800	12.7	2,886	0.3
Human services	77,860	41.1	206,744	181,883	88.0	21,616	10.5	3,245	1.6
International and foreign affairs	3,146	1.7	25,033	22,189	88.6	1,934	7.7	910	3.6
Public and social benefit	17,789	9.4	68,515	59,409	86.7	7,450	10.9	1,656	2.4
Religion-related	8,591	4.5	7,900	6,509	82.4	994	12.6	397	5.0
Mutual and membership benefit	579	0.3	2,333	2,199	94.2	130	5.6	4	0.2
Total	189,433	100.0	1,551,119	1,346,696	86.8	187,604	12.1	16,819	1.1

Source: GAO analysis of SOI data from Forms 990. | GAO-15-164.

Note: All percent estimates have 95 percent confidence intervals that are within +/- 2 percentage points of the estimate itself. We excluded a very small sample of unknown or unclassified charitable organization filers from our analysis. Therefore, the amounts may not equal the total due to this exclusion and to rounding. Total expenses broken out by program service expenses, management and general expenses, and fundraising expenses are only reported on the Form 990. Therefore, this table does not include Form 990-EZ filers.

End Notes

[1] For the purposes of this report, charitable organizations are those organizations which are tax exempt with regard to their charitable activities under section 501(c)(3) of the Internal Revenue Code (IRC). Charitable organizations are "corporations, and any community chest, fund, or foundations, organized and operated exclusively for religious, charitable, scientific, testing for public safety, literary, or educational purposes, or to foster national or international amateur sports competition, or for the prevention of cruelty to children or animals."

[2] GAO, *IRS 2015 Budget: Long-Term Strategy and Return on Investment Data Needed to Better Manage Budget Uncertainty and Set Priorities*, GAO-14-605 (Washington, D.C.: June 12, 2014).

[3] SOI data from years prior to 2011 are not included in this report because the reporting thresholds varied so much in these years that year-to-year comparisons of the data would be difficult to interpret.

[4] GAO, *Standards for Internal Control in the Federal Government*, GAO/AIMD-00-21.3.1 (Washington, D.C.: November 1, 1999).

[5] GAO, *Understanding the Tax Reform Debate: Background, Criteria, & Questions,* GAO-05-1009SP (Washington, D.C.: Sept. 1, 2005).

[6] GAO, *Tax-Exempt Sector: Governance, Transparency, and Oversight are Critical for Maintaining Public Trust*, GAO-05-561T (Washington, D.C.: April 20, 2005); GAO, *Tax-Exempt Organizations: Improvements Possible in Public, IRS, and State Oversight of Charities*, GAO-02-526 (Washington, D.C.: April 30, 2002).

[7] See appendix II for a full list of accepted charitable purposes for 501(c)(3) organizations.

[8] 26 U.S.C. § 501(c)(3); 26 C.F.R. § 1.501(c)(3).

[9] *Streamlined Application for Recognition of Exemption Under Section 501(c)(3) of the Internal Revenue Code.* Charities that meet certain requirements and have gross receipts of $50,000 or less and assets of $250,000 or less, may submit the 1023-EZ, an abbreviated version of the original form.

[10] This excludes certain religious organizations, such as churches and their auxiliaries and associations, which are recognized as tax exempt, but need not apply for tax exempt status.

[11] IRS Form 990, *Return of Organization Exempt from Income Tax.*

[12] Every organization that qualifies for tax exemption as an organization described in 501(c)(3) is a private foundation unless it falls into one of the categories specifically excluded from the private foundation definition. Organizations that fall into the excluded categories are institutions such as hospitals or universities and those that generally have broad public support or actively function in a supporting relationship to such organizations. When applying for charitable organization status, an applicant is presumed to be a private foundation unless it can demonstrate that it is not a private foundation. Private foundations are subject to certain tax consequences which do not apply to other charitable organizations. For more information on the tax treatment of private foundations, please see appendix II.

[13] Until the fall of 2014, EO also included the Customer Education and Outreach unit, which attempted to improve compliance by developing and delivering programs and products designed to help charitable and other exempt organizations understand their tax responsibilities. This unit was moved to Shared Services.

[14] State charity regulators vary by state and include state attorneys general, secretaries of state, consumer protection and licensing bodies, a bureau of investigation, and similar entities.

[15] Internal Revenue Manual (IRM) 9.5.1 Administrative Investigations and General Investigative Procedures (http://www.irs.gov/irm/part9/irm_09-005-001.html downloaded November 24, 2014).

[16] Gross domestic product is the market value of all goods and services produced within a country during a given time period. See Brice S. McKeever and Sarah L. Pettijohn, *The Nonprofit Sector in Brief 2014* (Washington D.C.: Urban Institute, October 2014); and Molly F. Sherlock and Jane G. Gravelle, *An Overview of the Nonprofit and Charitable Sector*, CRS-R40919 (Washington, D.C.: Congressional Research Service, Nov. 17, 2009).

[17] See Sarah L. Pettijohn, Elizabeth T. Boris, Carol J. De Vita, and Saunji D. Fyffe, *Nonprofit-Government Contracts and Grants: Findings from the 2013 National Survey* (Washington D.C.: Urban Institute, December 2013).

[18] Tax expenditure estimates do not incorporate any behavioral responses and thus do not represent the amount of revenue that would necessarily be gained if the tax expenditure was repealed. Changes in taxpayer behavior are taken into account when Treasury prepares revenue estimates for proposed legislation.

[19] According to the Congressional Research Service (CRS), the term 'nonprofit organization' refers to "an entity that is not intended to be a profit-making corporation. The term can be more precisely understood to mean an entity organized under the laws of a state, with its status and privileges determined under state law. Because the qualifications for nonprofit status vary among states, it is possible for the term 'nonprofit organization' to be broader than, narrower than, or identical to the term 'tax-exempt' organization. For a nonprofit organization to be exempt from federal income taxes, it must meet the statutory requirements found in the Internal Revenue Code and usually must file an application with IRS. Some organizations, including small 501(c)(3) organizations and qualifying religious organizations, are exempt from the application requirement." See Sherlock and Gravelle, *An Overview of the Nonprofit and Charitable Sector*.

[20] See Katie L. Roeger, Amy S. Blackwood, and Sarah L. Pettijohn, *The Nonprofit Almanac 2012* (Washington D.C.: Urban Institute Press, 2012).

[21] Tax-exempt organizations are organizations that have received tax-exempt status from the IRS under Internal Revenue Code sections 501(c)-exempt organizations, 501(d)- religious and apostolic associations, 501(e)-cooperative hospital service organizations, 501(f)-cooperative service organizations of operating educational organizations, 501(k)- child care organizations, 501(n)-charitable risk pools, 527-political organizations, and nonexempt charitable trusts and split-interest trusts. For more information about other types of tax exempt entities, see appendix II.

[22] IRS, *Data Book, 2011,* Publication 55B (Washington, D.C.: March 2012).

[23] Pub. L. 109-280, § 1223(b), 120 Stat. 780, 1090–1091 (2006) (*codified at* 26 U.S.C. § 6033(j)).

[24] See Matthew R. Madara, *IRS Working to Clear Exempt Organization Application Backlog*, Tax Notes Today (Aug. 20, 2014).Charitable organizations that have had their tax-exempt status automatically revoked must file Form 1023, *Application for Recognition of Exemption Under Section 501(c)(3) of the Internal Revenue Code* to have their tax-exempt status reinstated, even if the organization was not originally required to file the form. Certain charitable organizations can file for reinstatement using Form 1023-EZ, *Streamlined Application for Recognition of Exemption Under Section 501(c)(3) of the Internal Revenue Code.*

[25] Figure 4 does not include private foundations, or Form 990-N filers—which are smaller charitable organizations in terms of assets.

[26] Although the Form 990-EZ shows the amount of expenses by charitable organizations, it does not break out expenses into this group of categories.

[27] GAO-02-526.

[28] These figures represent sources and potential violations for tax-exempt organizations. The figures could not be broken out separately for charitable organizations because of limitations in the EO data. However, because charitable organizations are a significant portion of tax-exempt organizations (about 66 percent), we expect the relative proportions to be similar for the charitable organizations.

[29] Individual charitable organizations may file information returns, such as the Form 990 and Form 990-EZ. They may also file tax returns—such as the Form 990-T—for unrelated business income and Form 941 for employment taxes.

[30] Corporate tax returns exclude Form 1120S, *U.S. Income Tax Return for an S Corporation.*

[31] A section 501(c)(3) organization must not be organized or operated for the benefit of private interests, such as the creator or the creator's family, shareholders of the organization, other designated individuals, or persons controlled directly or indirectly by such private interests. No part of the net earnings of a section 501(c)(3) organization may inure to the benefit of any private shareholder or individual. A private shareholder or individual is a person having a personal and private interest in the activities of the organization.

[32] Although some audits with a written advisory re-enter the EO audit stream and will be re-examined at a later date, they are not tracked in the aggregate once they re-enter the audit stream. EO considered a special project to review the impact of written advisories, and it was included in the work plan for years 2013 and 2014. However, managers reported those cases were not worked, due to resource issues and other competing higher priority work. This project is also not addressed in FY 2015 work plan.

[33] Section 1220(a) of the Pension Protection Act of 2006 added new Internal Revenue Code subsection 501(q), which establishes standards that a credit counseling organization must satisfy to qualify for exemption under Code subsections 501(c)(3) or 501(c)(4).

[34] Internal Revenue Service, *Strategic Plan, 2014-2017*, http://www.irs.gov/pub/irspdf/p3744.pdf.

[35] For more information on difficulties we found in measuring compliance, see GAO, *Corporate Tax Compliance: IRS Should Determine Whether Its Streamlined Corporate Audit Process Is Meeting Its Goals*, GAO-13-662, (Washington, D.C.; Aug. 22, 2013) and *Tax Compliance: Better Compliance Data and Long-term Goals Would Support a More Strategic IRS Approach to Reducing the Tax Gap*, GAO-05-753 (Washington, D.C.; July 18, 2005).

[36] GAO, *The Results Act: An Evaluator's Guide to Assessing Agency Annual Performance Plans,* GAO/GGD-10.1.20 (Washington, D.C.: April 1998) and GAO, *Streamlining Government: Questions to Consider When Evaluating Proposals to Consolidate Physical Infrastructure and Management Functions*, GAO-12-542 (Washington, D.C.: May 23, 2012). Also, the Government Performance and Results Act of 1993 (GPRA), as updated by the GPRA Modernization Act of 2010, requires agencies to set results-oriented goals, to establish performance measures and related performance indicators with targets in meeting such goals, and to report progress. Pub. L. No. 103-62, 107 Stat. 285 (1993); Pub. L. No. 111-352, 124 Stat. 3866 (2011).

[37] Treasury Inspector General for Tax Administration, *Inappropriate Criteria Were Used to Identify Tax-Exempt Applications for Review*, 2013-10-053 (Washington, D.C: May 14, 2013).

[38] National Taxpayer Advocate, *Fiscal Year 2014 Objectives Report to Congress and Special Report to Congress*, IR-2013-63 (Washington, D.C.: July 16, 2013).

[39] For more on the operational test, see appendix II.

[40] See Form 1023-EZ, *Streamlined Application for Recognition of Exemption Under Section 501(c)(3) of the Internal Revenue Code.*

[41] Including schedules for different types of organizations, the Form 1023 has 26 pages.

[42] We did not assess the reasonableness of this sample plan because information in the sample plan was not sufficient for such a review. For example, the plan did not detail the reasonableness of the reliability factor choice, describe implementation of the sample, detail how the data would be analyzed, or show how the analysis would be presented.

[43] GAO, Partnerships and S Corporations: IRS Needs to Improve Information to Address Tax Noncompliance, GAO-14-453 (Washington, D.C.: May 14, 2014).

[44] Churches and governmental entities, as well as certain related organizations, generally do not have to file annual returns or notices. However, all tax-exempt organizations, including churches, must report unrelated business taxable income on Form 990-T, which currently cannot be filed electronically. In addition, tax-exempt political organizations must file Form 8872 periodically to report certain political contributions and expenditures. Form 8872 must be filed electronically only if the organization has, or expects to have, annual contributions or expenditures in excess of $50,000.

[45] Department of Treasury, *General Explanations of the Administration's Fiscal Year 2015 Revenue Proposals*, (Washington, D.C.: March, 2014).

[46] GAO-14-453.

[47] 26 U.S.C. § 6103(h)(2).

[48] A proposed notice of deficiency, also known as a 30-day letter, notifies the taxpayer of a proposed change in their tax. The letter offers the taxpayer the opportunity to appeal this change. A final notice of deficiency is the 90-day letter.

[49] GAO-02-526 and GAO-05-561T.

[50] Pub. L. 109-280, § 1224, 120 Stat. 780, 1091–1093 (2006) (*codified at* 26 U.S.C. § 6104(c)).

[51] Reporting on another piece of proposed legislation with a similar provision as that which was enacted in the PPA, the Senate Committee on Finance stated that by giving state officials "earlier access to information about the activities of certain section 501(c) organizations, state officials will be able to monitor such organizations more effectively and better protect the public's interest in assuring that organizations that have been given the benefit of tax-exemption operate consistently with their exempt purpose." The report also stressed the importance of maintaining the confidentiality of taxpayer data and stated the Committee's belief that it was important to extend existing protections against unauthorized disclosure to disclosures of charitable organizations' data. S. Rep. 108-11 at 43 (2003).

[52] IRS also makes public a list of charitable organizations that have had their tax-exempt status automatically revoked. Auto-revocations occur when an exempt organization fails to file the appropriate information return or notice three years in a row. This list does not include information about why an organization may have had its tax exempt status revoked for other reasons.

[53] The twelfth report of recommendations of the Advisory Committee on Tax Exempt and Government Entities (ACT), *Exempt Organizations: Leveraging Limited Resources in the Tax Administration of Small Tax-Exempt Organizations* (Washington, DC: September 12, 2013).

End Notes for Appendix I

[1] GAO, *Standards for Internal Control in the Federal Government,* GAO/AIMD-00-21.3.1 (Washington, D.C.: November 1, 1999

[2] GAO, *Understanding the Tax Reform Debate: Background, Criteria, & Questions,* GAO-05-1009SP (Washington, D.C.: Sept. 1, 2005)

[3] GAO, *Designing Evaluations, 2012 Revision*, GAO-12-208G (Washington, D.C.: Jan. 31, 2012).

[4] GAO, *Tax-Exempt Sector: Governance, Transparency, and Oversight are Critical for Maintaining Public Trust*, GAO-06-561T (Washington, D.C.: Apr. 20, 2005) and *Tax-Exempt Organizations: Improvements Possible in Public, IRS, and State Oversight of Charities*, GAO-02-526 (Washington, D.C.: Apr. 30, 2002).

End Notes for Appendix II

[1] Unless otherwise noted, all section numbers refer to the Internal Revenue Code.

[2] Certain farmers' cooperatives, shipowners' protection and indemnity associations, political organizations, and homeowners associations are wholly or partially tax exempt. 26 U.S.C. §§ 521, 526, 527, 528. Qualified tuition programs established by states (also called 529 plans) and Coverdell education savings accounts are exempt from federal income taxes. 26 U.S.C. § 529, 530. Income accruing to possession of the United States and political subdivisions thereof, states and political subdivisions thereof, and the District of Columbia, from any essential governmental function or public utility is not included in gross income and therefore not taxed. 26 U.S.C. § 115. Income earned by foreign governments and international organizations from investments in the United States is generally exempt from taxation. 26 U.S.C. § 892.

[3] 26 U.S.C. § 503(b).

[4] 26 U.S.C. § 502. These organizations are sometimes called feeder funds.

[5] 26 U.S.C. §§ 511–513.

[6] 26 C.F.R. § 1.501(c)(3)-1(b).

[7] 26 C.F.R. § 1.501(c)(3)-1(c).

[8] 26 U.S.C. § 508(a).

[9] 26 U.S.C. § 508(c); 26 C.F.R. § 1.508-1(a).

[10] 26 U.S.C. § 170. Gifts to certain mutual benefit organizations (veteran groups, nonprofit cemetery companies, and fraternal beneficiary organizations) that use the gift for charitable purposes are deductible.

[11] 26 U.S.C. §§ 2055, 2522.

[12] 26 U.S.C. § 3306(c)(8).

[13] 26 U.S.C. § 4421(2)(B).

[14] 26 U.S.C. § 403(b).

[15] 26 U.S.C. § 508(b). Organizations that are exempt from the application requirement are also exempt from this presumption.

[16] 26 U.S.C. § 4940.

[17] 26 U.S.C. §§ 4941, 4943–4945.

[18] 26 U.S.C. § 6033(c).

[19] 26 U.S.C. § 4942(j)(3); 26 C.F.R. § 53.4942(b)-1.

[20] 26 U.S.C. § 4942.
[21] 26 U.S.C. § 170(b)(1)(A)(vii), (b)(1)(F).
[22] 26 U.S.C. §§ 501(a), 401(a).

In: Charitable Organizations
Editor: Lynda Meyers

ISBN: 978-1-63482-600-6

Chapter 2

TAX ISSUES RELATING TO CHARITABLE CONTRIBUTIONS AND ORGANIZATIONS*

Jane G. Gravelle and Molly F. Sherlock

SUMMARY

Prior to the financial crises and subsequent recession, the value of tax benefits for charitable contributions and organizations was estimated to be around $100 billion per year. About half of this cost arose from the deductions for charitable contributions with the other half from exemptions of earnings of nonprofits. In 2010, the deduction for charitable contributions resulted in an estimated $40 billion in federal revenue losses. On average, endowment investments in 2009 experienced losses, meaning that the federal government did not lose revenues from exempting asset returns from taxation. By 2011, these returns on endowments almost recovered to their prior levels, although they fell to approximately zero for 2012. Over the longer run, however, they are likely to earn a substantial return.

This report provides an overview of recent changes affecting tax-exempt and charitable organizations, while also discussing issues that

---

* This is an edited, reformatted and augmented version of a Congressional Research Service publication RL34608, prepared for Members and Committees of Congress, dated March 13, 2013.

may be of legislative interest in the future. The Pension Protection Act (P.L. 109-280) included a number of restrictions related to charitable contributions as well as restrictions on tax-exempt organizations. These changes are briefly surveyed.

In addition to changes regarding the treatment of charitable contributions and tax-exempt organizations that have been made in recent years, several issues may be considered in future legislation. A number of provisions related to charitable contributions were extended temporarily as part of the tax extenders in the American Taxpayer Relief Act of 2012 (P.L. 112-240). Most of the charitable extenders were contained in legislation first introduced in 2001. Some provisions were enacted temporarily in 2005; further provisions and extensions occurred in 2006, in the Pension Protection Act. These extenders include an individual retirement account (IRA) rollover, liberalized treatment of gifts of food inventory and conservation property, and two more technical provisions.

Limitations on itemized deductions have been proposed as part of the Fiscal Commission's recommendation. President Obama's budgets have proposed limiting itemized deductions' value, including charitable contributions, to 28%. Other types of limits may be considered as part of tax reform.

The Patient Protection and Affordable Care Act (PPACA; P.L. 111-148), in response to concerns regarding charity care and community benefits provided by tax-exempt hospitals, imposed new regulations.

Other issues that may arise reflect concerns about donor-advised funds and supporting organizations and educational institutions' endowments. For donor-advised funds and supporting organizations, the main issue is whether and how minimum distribution requirements should be imposed, alongside other new regulations. The decline in educational institutions' endowments had raised concerns that such declines may lead to tuition increases, although these assets have largely recovered. New reporting requirements for small tax-exempt organizations, enacted under the Pension Protection Act (P.L. 109-280) may cause a number of noncompliant tax-exempt entities to lose their tax-exempt status.

INTRODUCTION

Historically, the value of tax benefits for charitable contributions and organizations was estimated to be around $100 billion per year. This figure fell in recent years due to the economic recession and slow recovery. Although revisions to the treatment of charitable contributions and tax-exempt organizations that receive these contributions have been made in recent years, a number of issues remain unresolved. A number of provisions related to charitable contributions have been enacted on a temporary basis as part of the "tax extenders," including an individual retirement account (IRA) rollover, liberalized treatment of certain gifts of inventory, and some other provisions. The Tax Relief, Unemployment Reauthorization, and Job Creation Act of 2010 (P.L. 111-312) extended these provisions through 2011. The American Taxpayer Relief Act of 2012 (P.L. 112- 240) extended most, but not all, of these provisions through 2013. The future of various charitable tax provisions beyond 2013 is uncertain.

This report also addresses a number of current policy issues relevant for various types of charitable organizations. Issues relating to donor-advised funds and supporting organizations, such as distribution requirements, remain relevant. Similar concerns about whether funds were being paid out at a high enough rate have also been directed at university and college endowments, where a combination of high returns and relatively low payout rates has led to rapid growth. Issues have also been raised about whether nonprofit hospitals provide enough charity care. The Patient Protection and Affordable Care Act (PPACA; P.L. 111-148) attempted to address some of these concerns by imposing new requirements on nonprofit hospitals while requiring the Secretary of the Treasury in conjunction with the Secretary of Health and Human Services to report to Congress on charity care provided by tax-exempt hospitals.[1]

The President's budgets proposed limiting the value of itemized deductions (which would include charitable contributions) to 28% of each dollar. The final report of the Fiscal Commission also recommended limiting the value of tax benefits associated with charitable contributions. A number of other proposals for caps or floors have also been made as a part of tax reform.

In addition to addressing the issues mentioned above, this report discusses the current tax benefits for tax-exempt and charitable organizations, reviews legislative changes that have taken place in recent years, and discusses potential future legislative issues. It focuses on deductions for charitable contributions, and on institutions that are generally eligible for deductible charitable contributions, such as social welfare organizations, educational institutions, nonprofit hospitals, and churches, along with conduits to those institutions such as private foundations, donor-advised funds, and supporting organizations.

CURRENT TAX BENEFITS

The tax system provides a series of benefits for tax-exempt and charitable organizations. The most widely estimated and discussed is the deduction for charitable contributions, which is estimated in FY2014 to reduce federal revenue by $46.4 billion.[2] This amount has declined compared with previous projects when most of the 2001 tax rates were made permanent.

Another important benefit is the exemption of earnings on assets from the income tax. As discussed below, although this benefit is difficult to estimate, it appears to be as large, and historically has been in the neighborhood of $50 billion per year. For universities and colleges, these benefits are several times as large as the savings by donors from deducting charitable contributions. The value, however, fell temporarily given the reduction in earnings yields during the recent economic slowdown, had largely recovered, but fell again in 2012.[3]

Charitable Contributions

Not all tax-exempt organizations can receive tax deductible donations, but religious, educational, social welfare, health, animal protection, and similar organizations are eligible. In recent years, several revisions to the treatment of charitable deductions have been made, both to expand benefits and address potential abuses. Some of the provisions that expand benefits have become part of the "extenders," provisions that are currently set to expire at the end of 2013.

Although charitable deductions are available to all taxpayers, individuals who take the standard deduction do not have a marginal tax incentive to give.[4] Slightly over one-third of taxpayers itemize; about 30% deduct charitable contributions. Individuals' contributions are, in general, limited to 50% of income for most charities, but are restricted to 30% for certain nonprofits, including non-operating foundations and institutions set up for the benefit of members (such as fraternal lodges). Individuals can contribute property as well as cash, and the contribution of appreciated assets has particularly beneficial treatment, since the value of most appreciated assets can be deducted without including the capital gains in income. (Some contributions of property are limited to the smaller of basis or fair market value, such as business inventory.) For that reason, gifts of appreciated property are limited to 30% of income for most general charitable organizations, and to 20% for organizations with more restricted giving limits, such as non-operating private foundations. Corporate contributions are limited to 10% of taxable income. Individuals can also deduct costs of volunteering for charitable purposes, including out-of-pocket expenditures, costs of using a vehicle, and travel costs when there is no significant personal element.

The treatment of charitable contributions has been of legislative interest. A series of proposals to expand charitable benefits were made in the past, beginning with President Bush's 2000 presidential campaign, and followed by a series of bills introduced in Congress (referred to as the Community Solutions Act and the CARE Act). The centerpiece of the initial proposal was to allow charitable deductions for non-itemizers. This provision, which was relatively costly compared to other proposals, was scaled back with ceilings and floors, and ultimately not adopted. A number of more limited proposals were considered and some were adopted, largely on a temporary basis (part of temporary provisions referred to as the "extenders" that are continually reauthorized). Proposals and enacted legislation placing restrictions on charitable contributions were largely motivated by potential abuses, which led to some changes in the law. These included the lack of documentation of cash contributions, but largely focused on gifts of property, where the valuation of the property or even the existence of a true gift may be questioned.

Broad reform proposals have also suggested restricting charitable deductions to make incentives more efficient, both from an economic and administrative perspective, by only allowing charitable deductions in excess of a floor. More recently, charitable contributions may be affected by overall limitations on itemized deductions through general tax reform.

Tax Exemption of Earnings

A less visible, but nevertheless important, benefit is that tax exemption allows organizations to accumulate assets without paying tax on earnings.[5] Estimates discussed below suggest that the revenue loss from this tax benefit may be larger than that associated with charitable contributions deductions. If charitable contributions were spent quickly, this benefit would be minimal. If contributions are held as assets and invested, the tax exemption may confer significant benefits. There are several ways in which donations are invested rather than spent. Some types of active tax-exempt organizations maintain assets in the form of endowments, particularly educational institutions. Private foundations are often originally funded with a large donation and pay out a small share of assets (required to be at least 5%, however). Two other types of institutions are similar to private foundations in that they do not directly engage in activities and accumulate assets from which they make payments: supporting organizations and donor-advised funds. All of these types of asset accumulating institutions have been the subject of legislative interest.

Prior to the recent recession, revenue losses associated with allowing organizations to accumulate assets tax-free had increased substantially with the growth of educational institution endowments. At some institutions, earnings were substantial relative to payout rates. During FY2007 (which ended in June 2007 for most institutions), approximately $25 billion would have been raised if endowment earnings alone were subject to the corporate tax.[6] This is more than three times as large as the revenue loss for charitable donations to all educational institutions, which was approximately $7 billion in 2007. The ratio of revenue cost of the asset earnings to charitable contributions is probably smaller for other types of nonprofits. Nonetheless, the revenue cost of exempting asset earnings for all charitable organizations was likely as high as $50 billion prior to the recession, about the same size as the cost of the charitable deduction.

Returns on educational endowments were -18.7% in FY2009 and -2.5% over the 2007 through 2009 three-year period.[7] Over the 10-year period, endowments earned a net return of approximately 4%. The recent economic downturn highlights how revenue losses associated with the tax-free accumulation of assets are susceptible to economic conditions. Revenue loss will fluctuate as returns to assets fluctuate.

For FY2011, however, endowment returns had largely recovered, and the lost revenue for endowment earnings for educational institutions was projected at $22 billion, with overall costs were close to their FY2007 values.[8] Returns, however, fell to virtually zero (-0.3%), due in part to large losses on international equities and small gains on domestic equities. These markets should eventually recover, however.

Congress also addressed some issues associated with tax-exempt organizations themselves. Some of this concern was directed at circumstances where tax deductible donations are made to organizations that act as conduits and do not have charitable activities. Private non-operating foundations, recipients of donations that make grants to active organizations, are required to pay out 5% of assets. Donor advised funds and supporting organizations, however, had no payout requirements. These organizations were the subject of legislative interest, not only because of concerns about payout rates, but also about the possibilities of using these organizations, which were not subject to self-dealing rules as restrictive as foundations, for private benefit. Some changes for these organizations were adopted, but major changes, such as payout requirements, were not in all cases; instead, Congress authorized Treasury studies and decisions in the aftermath of those studies is uncertain.[9]

EXPANDING BENEFITS FOR CHARITABLE CONTRIBUTIONS AND ORGANIZATIONS

Although numerous legislative proposals have been introduced since 2001 directly relevant to the charitable sector, few of these proposals have become public law. The American Taxpayer Relief Act of 2012 (P.L. 112-24) was the latest to continue most of the charitable extenders (through 2013). The 111th Congress extended through 2021 these charitable provisions that had been allowed to expire as part of the extenders package in the Tax Relief, Unemployment Reauthorization, and Job Creation Act of 2010 (P.L. 111-312). The charitable extenders, which had been allowed to expire at the end of 2009, had last been extended by the 110th Congress as part of the Emergency Economic Stabilization Act of 2008 (P.L. 110-343). The 111th Congress also enacted legislation to accelerate tax deductions for charitable contributions made to Haiti's earthquake victims.[10]

The 109th Congress enacted a number of pieces of legislation with provisions to promote charitable giving. Much of this legislation was aimed at disaster relief.[11] The Pension Protection Act of 2006 (P.L. 109-280) contained a number of provisions that restricted charitable giving, including new reporting requirements for tax-exempt organizations; new requirements on donor-advised funds, supporting organizations, and credit counseling organizations; and enhanced incentives for charitable giving, such as the tax-free distributions from IRA accounts for charitable purposes.[12]

This section summarizes the tax proposals liberalizing charitable contributions and briefly reviews the issues in most cases. It is followed by a section summarizing the tax proposals restricting charitable contributions and organizations. Each proposal considered in this section is identified as not adopted, temporary (adopted as a temporary provision without expectation of extension), extender (adopted with an expiration date as part of the extenders proposals), or permanent. Note that further details of provisions enacted are contained in the Joint Tax Committee's "Blue Books," that summarize legislation.[13]

Provisions Considered But Not Adopted

In recent years, a number of provisions have been included in various proposals, but ultimately have not been adopted. These include a deduction for non-itemizers, a reduction in the foundation excise tax, and an increase in the income limit on corporate deductions. However, a proposal to replace the disallowance of tax-exempt status for unrelated business income in a charitable remainder trust with an excise tax was adopted in 2006.

Deduction for Non-Itemizers

The most significant charitable contributions proposal, in scope and revenue, considered in recent Congresses was a deduction for non-itemizers. Under current law a taxpayer can either itemize deductions (the major deductions are charitable contributions, excess medical expenses, mortgage interest, and state and local income and property taxes) or choose the standard deduction. The standard deduction is advantageous if the amount of the standard deduction is larger than total itemized deductions.[14]

When President George W. Bush first proposed extending the deduction for charitable contributions to non-itemizers in 2001 no restrictions were imposed. Most legislative proposals contained some limitation on this deduction, either in the form of a cap (a limit on the amount that could be deducted) or a floor (where only contributions above a certain threshold could be deducted). Although a number of proposals were contained in legislation introduced in recent years, extending the deduction for charitable giving to non-itemizers has not been enacted. Although the 2006 Pension Protection Act (P.L. 109-280) did include a number of charitable giving incentives, a deduction for non-itemizers was not included in this piece of legislation.

Modifications to the charitable deduction have been proposed as part of broader tax reform or deficit reduction strategies. President Obama's Fiscal Commission recommended replacing the charitable deduction with a 12% nonrefundable tax credit available to all taxpayers.[15] Under this proposal, the credit would only be available for donations above a 2% of adjusted gross income (AGI) floor.[16] The 2005 President's Advisory Panel on Federal Tax Reform proposal on overall tax reform also included in its plans an extension of the deduction to non-itemizers, but added a floor of 1% of AGI, for both itemizers and non-itemizers.[17]

The Congressional Budget Office (CBO) has also discussed proposals to curtail the charitable giving deduction. A proposal that would limit deductions to donations above 2% of AGI for itemizers would generate an estimated $219 billion in additional revenues over 10 years.[18]

The CBO has also looked at extending the charitable deduction to non-itemizers. A non-itemizer's deduction with a $200 cap for married couples filing jointly ($100 for individual filers) would cost $8.2 billion over 10 years. A $500/$250 cap is estimated to cost $31.3 billion over 10 years.[19]

The main objective of extending the charitable deduction to non-itemizers was to increase charitable giving. Charitable provisions were, however, considered after the 2001 tax cuts which involved considerable revenue costs. Caps were seen as a means to constrain the revenue loss. At the same time, while the deduction for non-itemizers may increase giving, its effects would be limited because of the cap, and the dollars of charitable giving induced per dollar of revenue loss would be smaller, particularly with a small cap. In addition, the provision would increase complexity for taxpayers who do not itemize.

Floors also limit the revenue cost, but increase effectiveness per dollar of revenue lost (relative to a provision without a floor) and simplify the tax code because taxpayers with small amounts of contributions would not qualify. Even without a cap, the deduction may not induce additional giving as large as the revenue loss because the responsiveness of taxpayers, particularly lower and moderate income taxpayers, to incentives may be small.[20]

Reducing the Foundation Investment Income Excise Tax

Current law imposes a 1% tax on investment income of foundations, and an additional 1% if the foundation does not make a certain minimum distribution (based on average distribution rate over the previous five years), or has been subject to a tax for failure to distribute in the previous five years. Past legislative action has sought to remove the additional 1% tax.[21] Legislation introduced in the 111th Congress, H.R. 4090 and S. 676, would have set a single tax rate of 1.32% on the investment income of foundations.

Private foundations, whose contributors (or their families) retain the right to direct the distribution of funds, have been subject to greater scrutiny, in part because of the possibility of the donor (or family) obtaining a private benefit. Foundations are required to distribute 5% of their assets each year (or pay a penalty), but the tax is credited against that distribution.

If the foundation is just making the minimum distribution, every dollar of tax reduction should be funneled into distributions because the tax is credited against the deduction. Since the tax and the actual distribution sum to a fixed amount, a fall in the tax will result in a rise in the amount distributed to other organizations. Moreover, the moving average rule that imposes the additional 1% tax if the foundation does not distribute at the average rate of the last five years discourages a large contribution in a particular year because it increases the hurdle for future avoidance of the tax. Proponents of current proposals to impose a fixed 1.32% tax rate on the investment income of foundations highlight that doing so would remove the disincentive for foundations to make large one-time payouts, often necessary to address natural disasters and other crises.[22] The reduction in the investment tax should also make private foundations more attractive to givers in general, although that increased attractiveness might in part induce more contributions, and in part replace contributions that might have gone to other charities. The effects should be small, however, because the tax is small.

Proponents of reducing the tax also argued that it should be reduced because it brings in revenue that is in excess of IRS audit costs, which they indicate was the original purpose of the tax (which was introduced in 1969). The revenue stream from this tax has, however, been quite variable recently because it is heavily affected by the stock market. In any case, a reading of the legislative history indicates that while the Senate characterized the tax as an audit fee, the House referred more generally to the notion that private foundations should bear part of the cost of government generally because of their ability to pay (as well as viewing it in part as a user fee), and both objectives were cited in the bill's final explanation. It was reduced twice (in 1978 and 1984) based on the argument regarding costs of audit versus revenue.

Another argument made for eliminating the additional tax is the additional complication arising from it. At the same time, simplification does not require reduction in the tax; it could be converted to a larger flat fee.

Raising the Corporate Charitable Deductions Cap

Under current law corporations can deduct charitable contributions of up to 10% of income. Proposals introduced in the House in 2003 would have gradually raised the cap to 20% (by one percentage point each year beginning in 2004, reaching 15% in 2008-11, and 20% thereafter). The initial (107th Congress) provision would have raised the limit to 15%. This provision is relatively small, and most corporate giving already falls well under the cap; average giving is less than 2% of income.

Some question the appropriateness of corporate charity, since shareholders could make their own decisions about charitable giving. Allowing the deduction at the firm level is, however, more beneficial to the donor because both the corporate and individual taxes are eliminated. In some views, charitable giving by corporations is another management perk that might be excessive because of monitoring problems by shareholders (this problem is also called an agency cost problem). Others argue that corporations should be encouraged to give to charity and to be socially responsible. Economists have studied models in which charitable giving is part of the firm's profit maximizing behavior (e.g., by gaining the firm good will). Evidence on the effectiveness of the deduction is mixed, with time series studies showing a positive effect and cross section results not finding an effect.[23]

Unrelated Business Income of Charitable Remainder Trusts

Current law provides tax deductions for some portion of a trust and income tax exemption on the earnings, if a remainder of the assets is left to charity (while paying income to a non-charitable donee, usually a spouse or other relative during an interim period). The trust's income, however, was no longer exempt from tax if the trust had unrelated business income. An alternative to liberalize the rule by providing for a 100% excise tax on any unrelated business income rather than loss of all tax exemption was adopted in 2006.

Disaster Provisions Enacted on a Temporary Basis

Several provisions were enacted in 2005 in response to disasters. The Tsunami Relief Act of 2005 (P.L. 109-1) allowed contributions made in January 2005 to be treated as made in the previous year (and therefore deductible on 2004 tax returns) to encourage giving for relief from the Tsunami that struck in 2004. The Hurricane Katrina Emergency Relief Act of 2005 (P.L. 109-73) adopted several provisions, effective through 2005, to encourage giving to Katrina victims. It allowed unlimited cash contributions for individuals (normally restricted to 50% of income). It also allowed unlimited contributions for corporations (normally restricted to 10% of taxable income) if contributions were made to aid Katrina victims. Charitable contributions made after the disaster were not subject to the phase out of itemized deductions. Mileage rates for deducting costs of using a vehicle for charitable purposes to aid Katrina victims were increased from 14 cents to 70% of the business rate of 48.5 cents. Reimbursements for these costs in excess of the mileage allowance were not included in income if the activity was for the aid of Katrina victims. The Gulf Opportunity Zone Act (P.L. 109-135) extended the benefits of higher limits to contributions to Hurricanes Rita and Wilma.

In 2010, Congress passed the Haiti Assistance Income Tax Incentive Act (HAITI Act; P.L. 111- 126). This legislation contained provisions similar to those enacted following the Tsunami in 2004, allowing taxpayers to claim tax deductions for giving on the previous years' tax returns.[24]

Provisions Now Part of the Extenders[25]

A number of charitable provisions have been enacted on a temporary basis, and are now part of the tax extenders. The American Taxpayer Relief Act of 2012 (P.L. 112-240) extended five of the seven provisions through 2013, reinstating them retroactively for 2012. Previously, the Tax Relief, Unemployment Reauthorization, and Job Creation Act of 2010 (P.L. 111-312) retroactively extended all of the provisions, which had been allowed to expire at the end of 2009, through 2011. Prior to the most recent extension, the provision relating to donation of conservation property was last extended by the Food and Energy Security Act of 2007 (P.L. 110- 234). Six others, including the IRA rollover provision, three provisions relating to donations of business inventory, a provision regarding the effect of a charitable donation on the basis of stock of small corporations that elect to be taxed as partnerships, and a provision eliminating the unrelated business income tax on arms-length rental payments to tax-exempt organizations from a related entity were extended by the Emergency Economic Stabilization Act of 2008 (P.L. 110-343). The two provisions not extended by P.L. 112-240 were those for business donations of computer equipment and books.

Contributions of Conservation Property

Another important set of provisions, originated in the Senate, expanded benefits for contributions for conservation purposes by lifting the cap on contributions as a percent of income. Gifts of appreciated property are deductible at the fair market value, but, for individuals, have lower limits (30% of income) than ordinary gifts such as cash (50% of income). The Pension Protection Act (P.L. 109-280) increased the limit for appreciated property contributed for conservation purposes to 50% for individuals. The provision increased the limit to 100% for farmers and ranchers, including individuals and for corporations that are not publicly traded. To qualify, land used or available to be used for agricultural or livestock production must remain available for such purposes. This provision expired at the end of 2007, but was extended for an additional two years in the Food, Conservation, and Energy Act of 2008 (P.L. 110-234) and for another two years by the Tax Relief, Unemployment Reauthorization, and Job Creation Act of 2010 (P.L. 111-312). The latest legislation, the American Taxpayer Relief Act of 2012 (P.L. 112-240) extended this provision through 2013, at an estimated cost of $254 million. As noted above, lower income limits for gifts of appreciated property reflect concerns about the overstatement of fair market value and the deduction of amounts that have not been included in income.

IRA Rollover Provision

Currently, individuals aged 701/2 and older are allowed to make tax free distributions from individual retirement accounts to charities. This provision was adopted on a temporary basis in the Pension Protection Act in 2006 but expired at the end of 2007, and is now extended through 2011. The treatment benefits non-itemizers, who would not otherwise be able to take a deduction.

Although this treatment may appear no different, for itemizers, from simply including the amounts in adjusted gross income and then deducting them as itemized deductions, it can provide several types of benefits even to those who itemize. This treatment reduces adjusted gross income, which can trigger a variety of phase-outs and phase-ins, including the phase-in of taxation of Social Security benefits. There are also income limits on charitable contributions: individuals can contribute no more than 50% of income in cash and no more than 30% in appreciated property. Because IRAs tend to be held by higher income individuals, the taxpayers might be somewhat more sensitive to the incentive to give; however, the law does not specify why this particular group of taxpayers was targeted for an expansion of charitable giving provisions. This provision was adopted in P.L. 109-280 with a $100,000 annual limit. It was originally projected to cost $238 million in the first year and $856 million over 10 years. The latest two year extension in P.L. 112-240 has an estimated 10-year cost of $1.28 billion.

Extending the Deduction for Food Inventory to all Businesses

Corporations that donate inventory to charity in general get a deduction for the cost (not the market value). A special rule allows businesses paying the corporate tax to also exclude half the appreciation (half the difference between market value and cost of production) if the inventory is given to an organization that directly passes it on to the ill, the needy, or infants, as long as the total deduction is no more than twice the cost. An important category of donations is food. There have been disputes between taxpayers and the IRS about how to measure the fair market value of food.[26] The charitable contributions proposals would have allowed unincorporated businesses (or businesses that are incorporated but do not pay the corporate tax) the additional deduction, and the fair market value of wholesome food would be considered the price at which the firm is currently selling the item (or sold it in the past), although this deduction would be limited to the corporate percentage cap on deductions in general. This provision's cost was relatively small.

The provision's objective was to create more equity among different types of taxpayers and resolve disputes (largely in the taxpayer's favor). However, as with the deduction of appreciated property, these rules allow firms to deduct amounts that have not been included in income. Although the provision is limited by allowing only one-half the appreciation, these products, if sold, would be taxed at full rates (rather than the lower rates imposed on individual capital gains). In addition, as with gifts of capital gain property, an important concern is the potential overstatement of market value. Firms may only be able to sell donated inventory at a much lower price because the product is damaged in appearance, is older, or has other characteristics that would require deep discounting to sell. Moreover, a firm with market power may not wish to sell all of its inventory because increasing supply will drive the price down more for a sale than a donation. It is possible that a provision that is extended to non-corporate businesses, which are smaller and more numerous, will be more difficult to monitor for compliance.

For inventory that cannot be practically sold, the barrier to a donation by the firm is the extra costs encountered in distributing the product. Thus, there is a tradeoff between creating an incentive and providing a windfall for the firm.

The Katrina Emergency Relief Act of 2005 (P.L. 109-73) provided treatment to unincorporated firms (not to exceed 10% of business income) through 2005 but did not make the other changes. The Pension Protection Act of 2006 (P.L. 109-280) extended the provision through 2007, and the Emergency Economic Stabilization Act of 2008 (P.L. 110-343) extended it through 2009. The Tax Relief, Unemployment Reauthorization, and Job Creation Act of 2010 (P.L. 111-312) extended this provision through 2011. P.L. 112-240 extended it for an additional two years with an estimated cost of $314 million over 10 years.

Contributions of Computer Equipment

C corporations that donate computer technology or equipment to educational organizations or tax-exempt charities that support elementary and secondary education are eligible for a deduction. In concrete terms, this rule requires that no more than 50% of the cost is due to parts purchased elsewhere. The issues surrounding this provision are the same as those related to other contributions of inventory, such as food inventory.

The Tax Relief and Health Care Act of 2006 (P.L. 109-432) extended the provision for two years. Most recently, the Emergency Economic Stabilization Act of 2008 (P.L. 110-343) extended the provision through 2009. The Tax Relief, Unemployment Reauthorization, and Job Creation Act of 2010 (P.L. 111-312) extended this provision through 2011, with an estimated cost of $350 million over 10 years. This provision was not extended by P.L. 112-240.

Contributions of Book Inventory

A provision that originated in the Senate extended the treatment of food inventories to book inventories for C corporations that donated to public elementary and secondary schools. As with all contributions of property, valuation may be an issue. Book publishers who have printed too many books may only be able to sell them at a discount, and perhaps a potentially deep one. This provision was enacted in the Katrina Emergency Relief Act of 2005 (P.L. 109-73) through 2005.

The Pension Protection Act of 2006 (P.L. 109-280) extended the provision through 2007, and the Emergency Economic Stabilization Act of 2008 (P.L. 110-343) extended it through 2009. The Tax Relief, Unemployment Reauthorization, and Job Creation Act of 2010 (P.L. 111-312) extended this provision through 2011, with an estimated cost of $53 million over 10 years. This provision was not extended by P.L. 112-240.

Basis of S Corporation Stock for Charitable Contributions

Under current law, a shareholder in a Subchapter S corporation (a corporation treated as a partnership) is allowed to deduct his or her pro rata share of any corporate contribution. At the same time, the taxpayer must decrease the basis of stock by that amount (which is a way of reflecting the effect on the shareholder's asset position). The Congressional proposals on charitable contributions provided that the taxpayer would not have to reduce basis in the stock to the extent a deduction is taken in excess of adjusted basis of the donated property (e.g., cost). This provision appears to be consistent with allowing a deduction for the market value of appreciated property without including the appreciation in income (a special benefit generally available to taxpayers). This provision's cost was relatively small. The Pension Protection Act of 2006 (P.L. 109-280) included this provision effective through 2007, and the Emergency Economic Stabilization Act of 2008 (P.L. 110-343) extended it through 2009. The Tax Relief, Unemployment Reauthorization, and Job Creation Act of 2010 (P.L. 111-312) extended this provision through 2011. P.L. 112-240 extended this provision through 2013, with an estimated cost of $225 million over 10 years.

Unrelated Business Income: Related Party Payments

Charities are subject to a tax on unrelated business income. Rents, royalties and annuities are excluded from income subject to the tax except when received by a majority owned subsidiary. Among provisions included in the 108th Congress version of charity proposals was one to exclude certain items (such as rent) received by a subsidiary from a tax on unrelated business income except for the excess over an arms-length price. As with other provisions, however, the determination of arms-length rents is not always straightforward when there are not closely comparable properties. This provision was adopted in the Pension Protection Act (P.L. 109-280), and applied to payments through 2007. The Emergency Economic Stabilization Act of 2008 (P.L. 110-343) extended it through 2009. The Tax Relief, Unemployment Reauthorization, and Job Creation Act of 2010 (P.L. 111-312) extended this provision through 2011. P.L. 112-240 extended this provision through 2013, with an estimated cost of $40 million over 10 years.

Permanent Reduction in Excise Tax Reduction for Blood Collector Organizations

The Pension Protection Act of 2006 (P.L. 109-280) included a provision exempting qualified blood collectors from a variety of excise taxes, including communications taxes and taxes relating to fuels and vehicles. This provision is directed at the Red Cross.

RECENT RESTRICTIONS ON CHARITABLE DONATIONS AND ORGANIZATIONS

Congress has considered many provisions in recent years aimed at preventing potential abuse, with many problematic areas identified by the Internal Revenue Service.[27] The Senate Finance Committee has investigated many compliance issues.[28] In 2004 and 2005, the Senate Finance Committee held hearings on the subject. Also, early in 2005, the Joint Committee on Taxation published a study on options to improve tax compliance that included a number of provisions relating to charitable contributions and tax-exempt organizations.[29]

The concerns expressed in these hearings and studies focused on potential abuses of charitable organizations, on the valuation of gifts of property, and on certain types of organizations, including donor-advised funds and supporting organizations. These two types of organizations, like private foundations, permit contributions to build up an account without necessarily making a contribution. Private foundations, however, are subject to a 5% payout requirement and a number of special restrictions to prevent funds from being used for the benefit of the donor. Donor-advised funds are funds where the donor contributes to an account in an institution and the institution subsequently makes contributions, advised by the donor. Supporting organizations do not have a direct charitable purpose, but support organizations that do.[30]

More broad ranging proposals to make the charitable contributions deduction more effective and less subject to claims of small undocumented deductions would have introduced a floor. Earlier proposals associated with expansions of the deductions to non-itemizers proposed dollar floors, but these proposals tended to focus on floors as a percent of income. As noted above, the Deficit Commission's proposal would create a charitable credit available to all taxpayers, subject to a floor of 2% of income. The 2005 President's Advisory Panel on Tax Reform proposed a floor equal to 1% of income. The Congressional Budget Office included a budget option for a floor of 2%.

Some changes were enacted in 2003 and 2004, but most of the restrictive provisions that were adjusted were part of the Pension Protection Act of 2006.

Restrictions on Charitable Contributions

A series of restrictions on charitable donations, aimed at reducing abuse, were adopted in 2006. Most of these provisions related to gifts of appreciated property, where the gift is deducted at fair market value. These gifts account for about 25% of all donations, and for much larger shares of donations of higher income taxpayers. For taxpayers with incomes above $10 million, gifts of property account for 50% of contributions. Taxpayers with incomes above $1 million account for 18% of cash gifts, but 40% of property gifts.[31] This provision is especially beneficial to the donor because a deduction is allowed for the full value, while the appreciation is not taxed. While the valuation of contributions such as publicly traded stock is straightforward, the valuation of gifts where value is not easily assigned presents some issues for tax compliance. If the taxpayer can value donated property at an excessive value, it is even possible to benefit privately from making a contribution rather than by selling the property.

The President's Advisory Commission on Tax Reform proposed in 2005 that individuals be allowed to sell appreciated property and donate the proceeds without paying the capital gains tax, to address the valuation problem.[32]

During the debate on the treatment of gifts of appreciated property, some broad changes were discussed. For example, the Joint Committee on Taxation presented an option in its study to allow only the basis to be deducted for gifts of property that were not publicly traded. A Senate staff discussion paper, among a broad array of options discussed, considered "baseball arbitration," where the court can only find for the taxpayer's original value or the IRS value, which would create an incentive to limit any overstatement of value.[33] Although these provisions were not adopted, a number of changes were, as detailed below.

Vehicle Donations and Gifts of Intellectual Property

Growing concerns about the abuse of donations of used vehicles and of patents and other intellectual property led to several revisions in the American Jobs Creation Act of 2004 (P.L. 108- 357). According to IRS data, in 2003, $2.3 billion of deductions associated with vehicles was deducted, for those taxpayers who had non-cash contributions of $500 or more.[34] Often charities resold vehicles at a much smaller value than the value deducted by the taxpayer.[35] The revision required that, for vehicles with a value of $500 or more, the deduction is restricted to the value of resale, if the vehicle is resold rather than used or refurbished by the charity. The act also extended to corporations the requirement of an appraisal for a donation of property (other than readily valued property such as cash, inventory, and publicly traded securities) of $5,000. This appraisal is not required in the case of resale of a vehicle by an organization. It also required appraisals to be attached to tax returns for gifts valued at $500,000 or more. Finally the law restricted the donation of intellectual property, which could be valued at fair market value, to the lesser of basis (roughly cost of developing or purchasing) or market value.

Contributions of Historical Conservation Easements

As a general rule, a taxpayer cannot take a deduction for a partial interest in a property. However, gifts of conservation or historical easements (where the taxpayer restricts the use of property) may be made. Their value is the reduction in the value of the property due to the easement. One concern that arose was that taxpayers were making gifts of easements on historical facades (the front of the building), which involve an agreement not to change the facade, when the regulations in the historical district already imposed this restriction. Thus there could be no effect on property values. A provision in the Pension Protection Act required these easement to be limited to buildings but to apply to the entire exterior (not just the facade), and that an appraisal be supplied.

Contributions of Taxidermy Property

Press reports suggested that individuals involved in big game hunting were receiving deductions for contributing their mounted trophies at inflated prices which were often resold at a lower price.[36] In addition to the revenue effects, concern was expressed by environmental and animal rights groups. The Pension Protection Act restricted the deduction to the cost of mounting the trophy; thus, cost does not include the cost of hunting trips.

Recapture of Tax Benefit if Not Used for Exempt Purpose

The Pension Protection Act requires individuals who give gifts of appreciated property to be subject to a recapture tax if the property is not used by the organization for its exempt purposes and is sold within three years. If the property is sold in the same year, the donor generally deducts basis (cost); if sold after that year, the donor must include in income the difference between fair market value claimed and the basis.

Deductions for Contributions of Clothing and Household Items

Contributions of used clothing and household items present difficulties because these items are difficult and time intensive to value and audit. They are significant in value, however. In 2003, these contributions were estimated at $8.6 billion for those with $500 or more of non-cash contributions; clothing accounted for two thirds of the total.[37] The amounts would be larger if taxpayers with contributions of less than $500 in cash were included. The Pension Protection Act disallows the deduction for items not in good used condition or better and provides the Internal Revenue Service with broad authority to disallow deductions. Items valued more than $500 may be deducted if not in good used condition or better if accompanied by an appraisal. Household items do not include items such food, art, antiques, jewels and gems, and collections.

Recordkeeping Requirements

The Pension Protection Act changed the rule that allowed substantiation of small cash contributions by a written record or log. All cash contributions must be substantiated by a bank record (e.g., cancelled check) or receipt from the organization.

Contributions of Fractional Interests

Taxpayers could deduct contributions of fractional interests in art although they could not deduct a contribution of a future right to the art.[38] For example the taxpayer could contribute a 10% interest in an art work to a museum, and receive a deduction for 10% of the value of the art. The museum would have the right to possess the art for 10% of the year. There were several concerns about this tax treatment. First, a court decision (*Winokur v. Commissioner*) settled in 1988 found that physical possession was not required to make a fractional interest donation, only the right to physical possession.[39] The Internal Revenue Service challenged this case, but the court found for the taxpayer. As a result, individuals could keep art work in their possession, perhaps through their lifetimes, or even pass the property on to their heirs, while still securing a charitable contribution deduction. The second is a concern that the possession or display of the art by the museum itself enhances the market value of the work, effectively increasing the value of the art work, and the value of future deductions or sales compared to an outright gift. Another set of issues relates to estate taxes. Estate taxes can be reduced by a reduction in value due to minority discounts—the view taken by the courts that an ownership of a minority interest in an asset loses some value because of lack of control. The minority ownership does not, however, affect the value of the charitable deduction for income or estate tax purposes. The Pension Protection Act requires physical possession by the donee; requires the gift to be completed within 10 years or at the donor's death, whichever comes first; disallows fractional donation of a property that is not wholly owned by the donor, or the donor and donee for later gifts (the Secretary of the Treasury can make an exception if multiple owners donate similar fractional shares); and requires that subsequent fractional shares are limited to market value at the time of the original donation. If these restrictions are not met the tax savings from the deduction are recaptured with interest and a 10% penalty.

Penalties on Overstatements of Valuations

This provision lowered the thresholds for imposing penalties for overstatements of value for the income tax and understatement for the estate tax. It also established a separate penalty structure for appraisers.

Restrictions on Tax-Exempt Organizations

A few provisions were enacted during the 108th Congress that applied to tax-exempt organizations, but most provisions were enacted in the 109th Congress, primarily in the Pension Protection Act in 2006. Some of these provisions affect organizations that are tax exempt but are not charitable organizations.

Terrorist Activities

The Military Family Tax Relief Act of 2003 (P.L. 108-121) provided for automatic suspension of the tax-exempt status of organizations placed on the designated list of terrorist organizations or supporters of terrorism. Normally, suspension of tax-exempt status requires or permits administrative and judicial proceedings.

Leasing Activities

In a provision not directly affecting contributions or tax-exempt status, but which nevertheless might have consequences for tax-exempt organizations, the American Jobs Creation Act of 2004 also restricted the ability of parties leasing arrangements to obtain favorable tax treatment.[40]

Penalties for Tax-Exempt Organizations in Prohibited Tax Shelters

Some tax shelter operations require participation of a tax-exempt entity. This provision imposed penalties on exempt organizations that are a party in a prohibited tax shelter transaction. It was enacted in the Tax Increase Prevention and Reconciliation Act (P.L. 109-222) in 2006.

Life Insurance

Investments in life insurance are subject to beneficial tax treatment, including exemptions when assets are paid at death and deferral of tax on investment earnings. State laws restrict the holding of an interest in life insurance if there is no insurable interest (e.g., a relationship with the insured). Some states exempt charities from the insurable interest and some allow insurable interests for private investors if there is also a charitable organization involved. The Pension Protection Act does not directly affect these relationships but requires temporary reporting on life insurance arrangements by exempt organizations (for two years) and mandates a study of this issue by the Treasury Department.

Penalties and Penalty Taxes

A series of penalties applies to certain actions of charitable and tax-exempt organizations. The most punitive penalty for an inappropriate action, in general, is to revoke the exempt status. There are a series of intermediate sanctions that generally impose monetary penalties. An excess benefit tax applies to transactions of charitable welfare organizations (other than private foundations) and social welfare organizations. Private foundations are subject to taxes or penalties for self-dealing, failure to distribute income, on excess business holdings, for investments that jeopardize the charitable purposes, and for taxable expenditures (such as lobbying or making open-ended grants to institutions other than charities). The Pension Protection Act increased those taxes and penalties.

Credit Counseling Agencies

Nonprofit credit counseling agencies obtained tax-exempt status because their purpose was largely to educate and counsel consumers, and perhaps offer some tailored debt management plans as well. A rapid growth of tax-exempt credit counseling agencies occurred in the 1990s. Press reports and investigations suggested that there was widespread abuse and that these new firms were not primarily being used for educational purposes but were used to enroll individuals into payment plans. The Internal Revenue Service performed audits and revoked tax-exempt status for some agencies. The Pension Protection Act established a series of standards and requirements for exempt credit counseling agencies and treated debt management plans as an unrelated business, with earnings subject to the unrelated business income tax.

Expanding the Base for Imposing Foundation Excise Taxes

As discussed above, foundations are subject to excise taxes on investment income. The Pension Protection Act expanded the base to include additional types of income—such as income from financial contracts, annuities, and certain capital gains.

Defining Conventions or Association of Churches

A convention or association of churches is not required to file an information return and is subject to provisions generally applicable to churches. The Pension Protection Act specified that a convention or association of churches would not fail to qualify because there are individual members.

Information Reporting: Organizations Not Filing Annual Returns

Although exempt organizations are generally required to file information returns, certain organizations are exempt (these include small organizations, certain religious organizations and certain government related organizations). The Pension Protection Act, requires these organizations to report contact information to the Internal Revenue Service (i.e., organizational title, address) using the Form 990-N, also known as the e-postcard.[41] Organizations failing to file for three years will have their tax-exempt status revoked.[42]

Disclosure to State Officials

The Secretary of the Treasury is required to notify the appropriate State officer of a refusal to recognize an organization as a charitable one that may receive tax deductible contributions, revocation of that status, and the mailing of a notice of deficiency for certain taxes. Returns and records relating to this disclosure must be made available for inspection. This provision in the Pension Protection Act revises the rules for disclosure of tax information to state authorities, including the disclosure, upon request, of a notice of proposed refusal to recognize, revoke, or issue a deficiency, names and addresses of applicants, and associated returns.

Disclosure of the Unrelated Business Income Tax Return

Organizations are required to make information and application materials available for public inspection. The Pension Protection Act requires disclosure to be applied to the return reporting unrelated business income.

Donor-Advised Funds and Supporting Organizations

The Pension Protection Act authorized Treasury Department studies of donor advised funds and supporting organizations and made other changes to their status. Donor advised funds are funds where donors make contributions and the institution holding the accounts makes contributions to charitable organizations with the advice of the donor. Although the donor has no legal control, in practice the donor's wishes are likely to be respected. Supporting organizations do not actively engage in charitable activities but support organizations that do by contributing funds to them. Supporting organizations fall into three types: Type I controlled by the charitable organizations, Type II, controlled by the same entity controlling the charitable organization and Type III, related to the charitable organization. Type III organizations may support many charitable organizations.

These types of organizations had many features in common with private foundations, but were not subject to self-dealing rules and other restrictions (meant to prevent the donor from receiving a private benefit) or payout requires (meant to keep the organization from accumulating funds without paying out some amount for charitable purposes). There was some evidence that abuses were occurring and that, in some cases, little was being paid out. In addition to the mandated studies, other changes, including the following, were made.

Donor-advised funds eligible for charitable contributions were specifically defined in the law. They were prohibited from providing benefits to the donors, they were required to have a governance structure if grants were made to individuals (such as a scholarship fund), and contributions of closely held businesses had to be sold within a short period of time.

Supporting organizations must indicate which type they are and certain Type III organizations will eventually be subject to a minimum payout (with the Treasury Secretary making such a determination through issuance of regulations). In August 2007, the Treasury issued proposed regulations and invited comment, indicating the same minimum distribution rule applying to foundations (5% of assets) is expected to be applied.[43]

In general, the Pension Protection Act prohibits supporting organizations from making grants or loans, or paying compensation, to substantial contributors. Supporting organizations cannot receive contributions from persons who control the organization and from private foundations if the supporting organization is controlled by significant persons at the foundation. They are not eligible for the rollover treatment for individual retirement accounts (IRAs). Type III organizations must also file additional information and cannot support foreign nonprofits.

CURRENT ISSUES SURROUNDING CHARITABLE DEDUCTIONS AND ORGANIZATIONS

There are a number of tax issues regarding charitable deductions and tax-exempt organizations that may be of interest in the 113th Congress. The charitable extenders discussed above are set to expire at the end of 2013. The President's Fiscal Commission suggested modifying the charitable deduction as part of comprehensive tax reform to address the deficit and fiscal sustainability. President's Obama's budgets have proposed to limit the value of itemized deductions, including charitable contributions, to 28%. Limits on itemized deductions may be considered as part of income tax reforms.

In addition, there has been interest, as indicated by hearings and by activities of the Senate Finance Committee in the tax-exempt status of nonprofit hospitals and in university endowments. The Patient Protection and Affordable Care Act (PPACA; P.L. 111-148) imposed a number of new requirements on 501(c)(3) tax-exempt hospitals. The Finance Committee has also shown interest in specific tax-exempt organizations, such as media related ministries.

Provisions enacted under the Pension Protection Act continue to raise issues of interest to the tax-exempt sector. The findings of Treasury studies on donor-advised funds and supporting organizations may have broader implications for the charitable sector generally. In 2010, a number of small tax-exempt organizations had their tax-exempt status revoked after failing to meet information reporting requirements enacted as part of the Pension Protection Act. These issues are discussed in greater detail in the sections below.

The Extenders

Table 1 reports the expected revenue cost of extending each of the charitable provisions contained in the American Taxpayer Relief Act of 2012 (P.L. 112-240) There are two issues associated with these charitable benefits "extenders": whether they are effective or appropriate provisions, and, if so, whether they should be temporary when most of the provisions of the tax code are permanent. The specific issues associated with each of these provisions were discussed earlier.

Table 1. Charitable Provisions Among the Extenders

Provision	FY2013-2022 Revenue Cost of Extension (Millions of Dollars)
Tax-free distributions from IRAs for charitable purposes	$1,280
Charitable deduction for contributions of food inventory	$314
Special rule for S corporations making charitable contributions	$225
Increased contribution limit for contributions of appreciated real property for conservation	$254
Special treatment of certain payments to controlling exempt organizations	$40

Source: Joint Committee on Taxation, JCX-1-13, January 23, 2013.

One criticism that could be made of using temporary provisions for charitable purposes is that although the budgetary cost is smaller for a provision extended only a year at a time, the intention is to continue the provision. This practice causes the official projected budget deficits to be smaller than they will likely be, takes up the time of the Congress with considering the extenders, and creates some uncertainty for taxpayers.

On the other hand, an argument that could be made in favor of temporary provisions is that a temporary provision makes reconsideration of the merits and design of the provisions more likely. Evidence suggests, however, that relatively few temporary provisions have been revised. One exception is the R&D tax credit, which has been the subject of some major revisions. Nevertheless, it could be argued that the temporary nature of these provisions is conducive to better tax policy because provisions are reconsidered even though they are rarely revised.

Limiting Itemized Deductions

Various proposals have been put forth that would limit the tax benefits associated with charitable contributions. The Fiscal Commission recommended replacing the charitable deduction with a 12% nonrefundable tax credit, available only for contributions above 2% of income. President Obama's budgets have proposed limiting the value of itemized deductions (which would include charitable contributions) to 28% of each dollar. Thus, under the proposal, taxpayers in the top brackets (33%, 35%, and 39.6%) would have each dollar of deductions reduced by 28 cents on the dollar rather than a reduction based on their marginal tax rate (for example, 33 cents).

Although there has been concern expressed about the effect on charitable giving, especially during difficult economic times, the provision would not affect giving today if it does not go into effect immediately. In fact, enactment today of a future change would be expected to increase contributions as taxpayers seek to make contributions before the cap is imposed. Estimates of permanent effects on charitable giving from the 28% limitation suggest the effects would be relatively small, generally around 1%.[44]

The itemized deduction cap overall was projected to raise $584 billion over 10 years (FY2013- FY2022).[45] This estimate assumed that 33% would rise to 36% and the 35% tax rate would rise to 39.6% whereas the permanent rates adopted in the American Taxpayer Relief Act of 2012 (P.L. 112-240) only changed part of the 35% rate to 39.6%, so the gain would be smaller. Internal Revenue Service statistics suggest that charitable contributions account for about a quarter of itemized deductions at higher income levels.

Other potential limits on total itemized deductions or other tax expenditures that could become a part of tax reform, such as a dollar cap or a percentage of income cap.[46] In general, if the desire is to encourage charitable contributions, a floor would retain much of the incentive effect while a cap would eliminate it.

Nonprofit Hospitals

The Patient Protection and Affordable Care Act (PPACA; P.L. 111-148) imposed a number of new requirements on 501(c)(3) tax-exempt hospitals. Prior to the enactment of PPACA, the tax writing committees, and especially Senator Grassley, had shown interest in nonprofit hospitals. A major concern was the degree of charity care and whether nonprofit hospitals are providing benefits that justify their charitable and tax-exempt status. The Congressional Budget Office released a study in 2006 that found that nonprofit hospitals overall provided only slightly more charity care than for profit hospitals.[47] The Senate Finance Committee held hearings on the topic "Taking the Pulse of Charitable Care and Community Benefits at Non-Profit Hospitals," on September 13, 2006, and the House Ways and Means Committee held hearings on "The Tax Exempt Hospital Sector," on May 26, 2005.

In a staff discussion draft released July 18, 2007, by Senator Grassley, the following concerns were raised about nonprofit hospitals: establishing and publicizing charity care, the amount of charity care and community benefits provided, conversion of nonprofit assets for use by for-profits, ensuring an exempt purpose for joint ventures with for-profits, governance, and billing and collection practices.[48] Subsequently, on October 24, 2007, Senator Grassley authorized a round-table to discuss the draft. Also in July 2007, the IRS released an interim report on nonprofit hospitals, where they found that the median share of revenues spent on charity care was 3.9% and almost half of hospitals spent 3% or less. The average was 7.4%.[49]

Under PPACA, tax-exempt hospitals are subject to four new requirements.[50] First, hospitals will be required to conduct a "community health needs assessment" and adopt an implementation strategy to meet those needs.[51] Second, hospitals are required to written financial assistance and emergency care policies. Third, hospitals may not charge individuals eligible under the financial assistance policy more than the lowest amount charged to those with insurance coverage. Finally, hospitals are required to make reasonable efforts to determine if an individual is eligible for financial assistance before beginning extraordinary collections actions.

PPACA also requires the Treasury Secretary to review the community benefit activities of tax-exempt hospitals. Additionally, the Treasury Secretary, in consultation with the Secretary of Health and Human Services (HHS) will be required to report annually to Congress information on charity care, bad debt expenses, unreimbursed costs for services, and community benefit activities.

University and College Endowments

Universities and colleges are classified as charitable organizations eligible to receive deductible contributions, and, also, as tax-exempt entities, do not pay tax on their investments. As indicated above, prior to the financial crises and subsequent recession, the benefit of exempting endowment income of colleges and universities from taxes was estimated at around $25 billion. At $25 billion, this exemption was worth more than three times the benefit of charitable deductions to all educational institutions. Historically, these high yields were coupled with relatively low payout rates. For the fiscal year that ended June 2007, endowments were $411 billion and the average rate of return was 21.5%. The payout rate was 4.6%. As a result of those relationships along with contributions, endowments grew 18.4% between FY2006 and FY2007 (about thee and a half times the growth rate of the economy), continuing an ongoing trend from recent years.

The losses in college and university endowment funds experienced during the recession have raised new issues of concern. In FY2009, losses were 18.7% on average.[52] Prior to the onset of the recession, Senator Grassley, ranking member of the Finance Committee, discussed concern that colleges were not using enough of their endowments funds to provide an affordable education.[53] Tuition rates remain an issue of interest. In 2010, following the release of data on college and university endowment losses, Senator Grassley noted:[54]

> I hope colleges won't rely on double-digit losses as a reason to raise tuition or freeze student aid. Many of them relied on some risky investments, like hedge funds, to get big gains in recent years, and now those strategies are causing losses. ... Pay-out rates over the last decade rarely topped 5 percent, even when investment returns were in double digits.

Donor-Advised Funds and Supporting Organizations

The two basic issues associated with donor-advised funds and supporting organizations were possibilities of receiving private benefit by donors and payout rates. As noted above, while some changes were enacted, others remain possible. Although payout requirements are planned (administratively) for Type III supporting organizations, there are no payout requirements for donor-advised funds and for other supporting organizations. These issues might be revisited when Treasury completes its studies.[55]

The Treasury was directed to study specific issues: whether deductions for contributions to donor-advised funds and supporting organizations are appropriate given the use of the assets or benefits to the donor, whether donor-advised funds should have a distribution requirement, whether the retention of rights by donors means that the gift is not completed, and whether these issues apply to other charities or charitable donors.

This Treasury study provided considerable data but it is not clear what policy implications should be. A CRS report that reviewed the study and updated the data in the case of donor-advised funds indicated that aggregate payout requirements for the overall fund would not have much effect, and that an effective payout requirement would need to be applied to each individual account. It also suggested, although the data are limited, that many accounts do not pay out contributions.[56]

Reporting Requirements and Exempt Status Revocation

The Pension Protection Act of 2006 implemented new reporting requirements for tax-exempt organizations with revenues of less than $25,000.[57] Entities failing to file required information returns (Form 990-N, also known as the e-postcard) with the IRS for three consecutive years will have their tax-exempt status revoked. Thus, revocations took place for the first time in 2010.

There are more than 714,000 tax-exempt organizations registered with the IRS that would be subject to new reporting requirements. As of July 2010, 41% of these organizations had yet to file.[58] There are various reasons why registered tax-exempt organizations may not file the required information returns. Some of these organizations may no longer exist. The required filings will help the IRS determine which organizations remain active. On the other hand, active organizations may not file if they are not aware of the new filing requirements. The IRS extended the filing deadline to October 15, 2010 to give charities that would have been required to file earlier in the year more time to comply with this new law. Further, the IRS has posted a list of organizations in danger of losing their tax-exempt status on their website.[59]

Specific Sectors Including Media-Based Ministries

Over a period of time the Senate Finance Committee has examined specific charitable organizations or groups as well as specific charitable donation practices. Some of these investigations were spurred by media reports and some by IRS studies; they have led to both legislation and self-correction by entities involved.

In 2007, Senator Grassley sent inquiries to several media-based ministries for information on their finances. Religious organizations do not have to file the information (990) forms that other tax-exempt organizations have to file, so generally it is difficult to obtain information on the activities of these tax-exempt entities. The results of this inquiry were announced on January 6, 2011. While not all ministries provided the requested information, enough information was gathered for Senator Grassley to determine that internal reforms were taking place.[60]

End Notes

[1] For more information, see CRS Report RL34605, 501(c)(3) Hospitals and the Community Benefit Standard, by Erika K. Lunder and Edward C. Liu.

[2] Joint Committee on Taxation, Estimates of Federal Tax Expenditures for Fiscal Years 2011-2015, JCS-1-13, February 1, 2013. The categories for education and health are estimated separately at $6.2 billion and $4.6 billion, respectively. In 2011, of overall charitable contributions, not all of which are deductible because they are made by non-itemizers, almost a third (32%) are to religious organizations, 13% are to education, 12% to human services, 9% to grantmaking foundations, 8 % respectively to health and international, 7% to public society benefit, 4% to arts, culture and humanities, 3% to environment and animals, 3% unallocated, and 1% grants from foundations to individuals. Reported on the National Park Service website, data from Giving USA 2012, at http://www.nps.gov/partnerships/ fundraising_individuals_statistics.htm.

[3] See data from National Association of College and University Business Officers (NACUO)–Commonfund study at http://www.nacubo.org/Research/NACUBO-Commonfund_Study_of_Endowments/Public_NCSE_Tables.html.

[4] The standard deduction does not impose a penalty, as it is an option that can be used when it is greater than the total sum of itemized deductions.

[5] The unrelated business income tax, or UBIT, is imposed on business activities unrelated to the charitable purpose, but it does not apply to investment earnings such as dividends and interest.

[6] For FY2007 (ending in June of 2007) endowments of universities totaled $411 billion, and earned a return of 21.5% according to the National Association of College and University Business Officers (posted at http://www.nacubo.org/ x2376.xml). At a 35% tax rate, this amount totals to $31 billion ($411 billion times 0.215 times 0.35). Based on the allocation of assets (about 60% to 70% in equity investments), standard shares in capital gains (60%) and shares of gains unrealized (50%), about 20% would be unrealized capital gains. The total loss would be about $25 billion ($31 billion times 0.80). The only other readily available data source of assets and earnings of specific charities is in the survey of large charitable institutions in the Chronicle of Philanthropy ("Special Report: Jitters Among Strong Returns," pp. 6-11, June 24, 2008). Adding the assets of institutions outside of education indicated that these large noneducational institutions had endowments about 40% the size of all educational institutions, with about three quarters attributable to foundations, implying an additional revenue cost of around $10 billion, for a total of $35 billion. This

estimate is incomplete, however, as only a limited number of charities are included and not all income is from endowments. For a more comprehensive number, some estimates of passive income are included in the national income accounts. Earnings for educational institutions for FY2006, a year with comparable data, were $52 billion. Although the income concepts are not precisely the same, in calendar year 2005 (which ended approximately six months earlier) total rents, dividends and interest reported in the National Income and Product Accounts ascribed to nonprofits and retained were $64 billion (Mark Ledbetter, Comparison of BEA Estimates of Personal Income with IRS Estimates of AGI, Survey of Current Business, November 2008, p. 38) and, if the share of capital gains were assumed to be the same as endowment investments, total income would be $106 billion, with the total for all nonprofits roughly twice the amount of educational institution endowment earnings. Hence, the total revenue cost would be about twice as large as the loss from exempting endowments, or about $50 billion.

[7] National Association of College and University Business Officers, "Educational Endowments Returned -18.7% in FY2009," press release, January 28, 2010, available at http://www.nacubo.org/Documents/research/ 2009_NCSE_Press_Release.pdf.

[8] Educational endowments were $417.4 billion, and the rate of return was 19.2% in FY2011. See data and press release at NACUBO, http://www.nacubo.org/Documents/research/ 2011NCSEPublicTablesEndowmentMarketValues319.pdf and http://www.nacubo. org/ Documents/research/2011_NCSE_Press_Release_Final_Embargo_1_31_12.pdf. However, the return fell to virtually zero for GY2012.

[9] See CRS Report R42595, An Analysis of Charitable Giving and Donor Advised Funds, by Molly F. Sherlock and Jane G. Gravelle, for a discussion of the Treasury Report and further analysis of data.

[10] For additional background, see CRS Report R41036, Charitable Contributions for Haiti's Earthquake Victims, by Molly F. Sherlock.

[11] See the Tsunami Relief Act of 2005 (P.L. 109-1), the Katrina Emergency Relief Act of 2005 (P.L. 109-73), and the Gulf Opportunity Zone Act of 2005 (P.L. 109-135).

[12] A detailed summary of the charitable provisions in the Pension Protection Act of 2006 from the Committee on Ways and Means is available at http://waysandmeans.house.gov/ media/pdf/taxdocs/072806charitable.pdf.

[13] These documents can be found on the Joint Committee's website http://www.jct.gov/. The legislation discussed in this report is summarized in two volumes: General Explanation of Tax Legislation Enacted in the 108th Congress, JCS-1-05, General Explanation of Tax Legislation Enacted in the 109th Congress, JCS-1-07, and General Explanation of Tax Legislation Enacted in the 110th Congress, JCS-1-09.

[14] Non-itemizers were allowed a limited deduction for charitable contributions from 1981-1986, a provision which was enacted as part of the Economic Recovery Act of 1981 (P.L. 97-34).

[15] The National Commission on Fiscal Responsibility and Reform, The Moment of Truth, December 2010, http://www.fiscalcommission.gov/news/moment-truth-report-national-commission-fiscal-responsibility-and-reform.

[16] Congressional Budget Office, Budget Options: Volume 2, August 2009, p. 193, http://www.cbo.gov/ftpdocs/102xx/ doc10294/08-06-BudgetOptions.pdf.

[17] U.S. Government Printing Office, President's Advisory Panel on Federal Tax Reform, Simple, Fair and Pro-Growth: Proposals to Fix America's Tax System, November 2005.

[18] Congressional Budget Office, Reducing the Deficit: Spending and Revenue Options, March 2011, p. 150. http://www.cbo.gov/sites/default/files/cbofiles/ftpdocs/120xx/doc12085/03-10-reducingthedeficit.pdf.

[19] Congressional Budget Office, Budget Options: Volume 2, August 2009, p. 195, http://www.cbo.gov/ftpdocs/102xx/ doc10294/08-06-BudgetOptions.pdf.

[20] See CRS Report RL31108, Economic Analysis of the Charitable Contribution Deduction for Non-Itemizers, by Jane G. Gravelle. The effects of alternative approaches on revenues and charitable giving were also addressed in Congressional Budget Office, Effects of Allowing Nonitemizers to Deduct Charitable Contributions, December 2002.

[21] A 2003 House proposal added a new provision that limited the counting of administrative costs as part of a foundation's minimum distribution requirement. Foundations are required to make a minimum distribution of 5%, but that 5% can currently include administrative costs (which currently have to be "reasonable"). As originally introduced earlier in 2003, the provision would have disallowed any administrative costs, but the proposal as reported allowed deductions for most administrative costs, with some exceptions. This provision was not enacted.

[22] Stephanie Strom, "Senate Measure Seeks to Spur Foundations to Give More," New York Times, March 25, 2009, Late Edition.

[23] See James R. Boatsman and Sanjay Gupta, "Taxes and Corporate Charity: Empirical Evidence from Micro-Level Panel Data," National Tax Journal, vol. 49, June 1996, pp. 193-213.

[24] For additional background, see CRS Report R41036, Charitable Contributions for Haiti's Earthquake Victims, by Molly F. Sherlock.

[25] More information on the extenders can be found in CRS Report RL32367, Certain Temporary Tax Provisions that Expired in December 2009 ("Extenders"), by James M. Bickley.

[26] See CRS Report RL31097, Charitable Contributions of Food Inventory: Proposals for Change, by Pamela J. Jackson.

[27] See, for example, testimony of Mark Everson, Commissioner of Internal Revenue, Statement on Exempt Organizations, Enforcement Problems, Accomplishments and Future Directions before the Senate Finance Committee, April 5, 2005, at http://finance.senate.gov/hearings/ testimony/2005test/metest040505.pdf.

[28] Summary of Senator Chuck Grassley's Non-Profit Oversight, November 20, 2007, at http://finance.senate.gov/newsroom/ranking/release/?id=83f6b20e-3327-4619-8b92-36ce643ef5fe.

[29] Joint Committee on Taxation, Options to Improve Tax Compliance and Reform Tax Expenditures, JCS-2-05, January 27, 2005, at http://www.jct.gov/s-2-05.pdf.

[30] Issues surrounding supporting organizations and donor-advised funds, as well as gifts of appreciated property, are discussed in the testimony of Jane G. Gravelle, on Charities and Charitable Giving: Proposals for Reform, before the Senate Finance Committee, April 5, 2005, at http://finance.senate.gov/imo/media/doc/jgtest040505.pdf.

[31] These data are reported in the testimony of Jane G. Gravelle, on Charities and Charitable Giving: Proposals for Reform, before the Senate Finance Committee, April 5, 2005, at http://finance.senate.gov/hearings/testimony/2005test/ jgtest040505.pdf.

[32] U.S. Government Printing Office, President's Advisory Panel on Federal Tax Reform, Simple, Fair and Pro-Growth,: Proposals to Fix America's Tax System, November 2005.

[33] For a discussion, see the testimony of Jane G. Gravelle, on Charities and Charitable Giving: Proposals for Reform, before the Senate Finance Committee, April 5, 2005, at http://finance.senate.gov/hearings/testimony/2005test/ jgtest040505.pdf.

[34] Janette Wilson and Michael Strudler, "Individual Non-Cash Charitable Contributions 2003," Internal Revenue Service, Statistics of Income Bulletin, spring 2006, p. 59.

[35] See, for example, the report by the GAO, Vehicle Donation: Benefits to Charities and Donors but Limited Program Oversight, GAO-04-73, November 2003, at http://www.gao.gov/new.items/d0473.pdf.

[36] See Zachary A. Goldfarb, "Pension Bill Also Curbs Hunter's Breaks," Washington Post, August 5, 2006.

[37] Janette Wilson and Michael Strudler, "Individual Non-Cash Charitable Contributions 2003," Internal Revenue Service, Statistics of Income Bulletin, spring 2006, p.59.

[38] The magnitude of these donations is difficult to determine as is the degree of potential abuse. Certain museums that had wealthy patrons using this process could lose significant donations, although these art works may not necessarily be exhibited constantly because of fractional ownership. According to a news report, the San Francisco Museum of Modern Art received 48% of donations in fractional giving in the fiscal year ending in 2001, although the share fell to 10% the next year and has recently climbed to 20% (See Sarah Duxbury, "SFMOMA Turns 'Timeshare' Gifts into an Art Form," San Francisco Business Times, August 19, 2005). In general, most discussions of fractional giving in the news seem to suggest that having the donor keep the art is not uncommon. (See Rachel Emma Silverman, "Joint Custody for your Monet," Wall Street Journal Online, July 7, 2007). A law journal article, in discussing the proposal to require physical possession stated: "This would effectively put an end to fractional gifts of large sculptures that are difficult and expensive to move every year. It will also substantially curtail fractional gifts of paintings since it is usually not the best idea to constantly move a fragile painting every year." This discussion also suggests that physical possession is an important issue. See Ralph E. Lerner, "Fractional Gifts of Art." New York Law Journal, April 24, 2006. A New York Times article stated "in practice, many museums have waived their right to possess pieces at all except when they needed them for exhibitions." Jeremy Kahn, "Museums Fear Tax Law Changes on Some Donations," New York Times, September 13, 2006.

[39] Winokur v. Commissioner, 90 T.C. 733 (1988), James Winokur contributed fractional interests in paintings to the Carnegie Museum, and the museum had a right to possess the paintings but never did. This case is summarized in Marylynne Pitz, "Fractional Donations Require Close Look at the Law," Pittsburgh Post-Gazette, July 24, 2005: http://www.postgazette.com/pg/05205/541620.stm.

[40] A discussion of this issue can be found in CRS Report RL32479, Tax Implications of SILOs, QTEs, and Other Leasing Transactions with Tax-Exempt Entities, by Maxim Shvedov. (Out of print; available from the author.)

[41] More information is available from the Internal Revenue Service at http://www.irs.gov/charities/article/0,,id=169250,00.html.

[42] The Internal Revenue Service provides answers to frequently asked questions regarding automatic revocation of tax-exempt status for entities failing to file informational returns. This information is available at http://www.irs.gov/ charities/article/0,,id=221600,00.html.

[43] For more information, see IRS Notice 2007-21, available at http://www.irs.gov/pub/irs-drop/n-07-21.pdf.

[44] CRS Report R40518, Charitable Contributions: The Itemized Deduction Cap and Other FY2011 Budget Options, by Jane G. Gravelle and Donald J. Marples. Paul N. Van de Water, Proposal to Cap Deductions for High Income Households Would Reduce Charitable Deductions by Only About 1%, Center on Budget Policy and Priorities, http://www.cbpp.org/cms/index.cfm?fa=view&id=2700. "How Changes in Tax Rates Might Affect Itemized Charitable Giving, by Deb Partha and Mark O. Wilhelm, The Center on Philanthropy at

Indiana University found a reduction of less than 1%, http://www.philanthropy.iupui.edu/docs/2009/ 2009_TaxChangeProposal_WhitePaper.pdf.

45 Department of the Treasury, General Explanations of the Administration's Fiscal Year 2013 Revenue Proposals, February 2012, at http://www.treasury.gov/resource-center/tax-policy/Documents/General-Explanations-FY2013.pdf.

46 See, for example, the proposal by Martin Feldstein, to cap benefits from certain tax expenditures, including itemized deductions, at 2% of income. Martin Feldstein "Raise Taxes, Not Tax Rates," New York Times, May 4, 2011, at http://www.nber.org/feldstein/nyt05042011.html.Governor Romney also discussed the possibility of dollar caps on deductions during the 2012 Presidential campaign. See Richard Rubin, "Romney $17,000 Deduction Limit Part of Three-Cap Concept," Bloomberg, October 4, 2012, at http://www.bloomberg.com/news/2012-10-03/romney-17-000- deduction-cap-first-of-three-part-proposal.html.

47 Congressional Budget Office, Nonprofit Hospitals and the Provision of Community Benefits, December 2006.

48 Tax Exempt Hospitals: Discussion Draft, at http://finance.senate.gov/press/Gpress/ 2007/prg071907a.pdf.

49 Internal Revenue Service, Hospital Compliance Program Interim Report, at http://www.irs.gov/pub/irs-tege/ eo_interim_hospital_report_072007.pdf.

50 For additional background, see CRS Report RL34605, 501(c)(3) Hospitals and the Community Benefit Standard, by Erika K. Lunder and Edward C. Liu.

51 This provision becomes effective for taxable years starting after March 23, 2012.

52 National Association of College and University Business Officers, Commonfund Study of Endowments, available at http://www.nacubo.org/Research/NACUBO_ Endowment_Study.html.

53 Charles E. Grassley, "Wealthy Colleges Must Make Themselves More Affordable," Chronicle of Higher Education, May 29, 2008, http://finance.senate.gov/newsroom/ranking/release/?id=c1b59ac6-5fb9-4770-8050-10c4e99d8b1e.

54 Office of Senator Grassley, "Grassley: Students, Families Shouldn't Bear Brunt of College Endowment Losses," press release, January 27, 2010, http://grassley.senate.gov/news/Article.cfm?customel_dataPageID_1502=24983.

55 See Nick Tarlson, "Donor Advised Funds: Prepare for Closer Scrutiny," Journal of Accountancy, 2008, http://www.aicpa.org/pubs/jofa/jan2008/donor_advised_funds.htm.

56 See CRS Report R42595, An Analysis of Charitable Giving and Donor Advised Funds, by Molly F. Sherlock and Jane G. Gravelle.

57 The IRS website provides details on the information tax-exempt entities are required to report to be in compliance with this new law. See http://www.irs.gov/charities/ article/0,,id=177792,00.html.

58 Amy Blackwood and Katie L. Roeger, Here Today, Gone Tomorrow: A Look at Organizations that May Have Their Tax-Exempt Status Revoked, The Urban Institute: National Center for Charitable Statistics, July 8, 2010, http://www.urban.org/Uploaded PDF/412135-tax-exempt-status.pdf.

59 See http://www.irs.gov/charities/article/0,,id=225889,00.html.

60 For additional information and access to the full reports, see The Office of Senator Grassley, "Grassley Releases Review of Tax Issues Raised by Media-based Ministries," press release, January 6, 2011, http://grassley.senate.gov/ news/Article.cfm?customel_dataPage ID_1502=30359.

INDEX

M

N

O

P

Q

R

U

V

W